AN INTRODUCTION TO CELEBRITY PROTECTION AND TOURING

ABOUT THE AUTHORS

Elijah J. Shaw is the CEO of ICON Global, Inc. A consulting firm specializing in Executive and VIP Protection. With tours of duty that frequently take him across the globe, Mr. Shaw acts as a personal bodyguard to several highly recognizable public figures, providing security consultation and staffing worldwide. As an instructor, Elijah teaches an internationally recognized program on Celebrity & VIP Protection at the ICON academy, as well as in conjunction with Executive Security International (ESI), the nation's oldest bodyguard school, where he currently sits on the Board of Directors. Elijah also serves as the current National Director of the North American Bodyguard Association (NABA) and holds the position of Managing Editor of the NABA-produced *Circuit Magazine* in which he writes an ongoing column entitled, *Keeping Your Edge*. A seasoned expert with dealing with the media on topics related to Executive Protection and the Bodyguard Industry, Elijah has been featured in prestigious publications such as *Portfol-io, Entrepreneur* and *Inc. Magazine*. In addition, he has been interviewed for his expert opinion on major broadcast such as *The Today Show, FOX* and *E! News*. On the philanthropic side, Mr. Shaw is the founder of *ISC Safety-Net,* a program that provides free security services to victims of domestic abuse and the shelters that support them.

Dale L. June (MA) former U.S. Secret Service Agent, Presidential Protective Division at the White House serving under three U.S. Presidents. With a distinguished career of service that has included City Police Officer, Military Policeman, U.S. Customs Intelligence Specialist, University Professor, and Author. An educator and teacher, Dale holds a M.A. Degree in Criminal Justice from George Washington University as well as a B.A. Degree in Public Administration, from Sacramento State University. Dale was inducted in the U.S. Martial Artist's Hall of Fame - Martial Artist of the Year (2005). Other books by Dale June: *Introduction to Executive Protection: Protection, Security and Safeguards: Practical Approaches and Perspectives; Terrorism and Homeland Security: Perspectives, Thoughts, and Opinions; The ReEvolution of American Street Gangs; What They Didn't Teach at The Academy: Topics, Stories and Reality Beyond the Classroom.*

AN INTRODUCTION TO CELEBRITY PROTECTION AND TOURING

A Guide to Mastering the Business of VIP Security

By

ELIJAH SHAW

and

DALE JUNE

CHARLES C THOMAS • PUBLISHER • LTD.
Springfield • Illinois • U.S.A

Published and Distributed Throughout the World by

CHARLES C THOMAS • PUBLISHER, LTD.
2600 South First Street
Springfield, Illinois 62704

This book is protected by copyright. No part of
it may be reproduced in any manner without written
permission from the publisher. All rights reserved.

© 2019 by CHARLES C THOMAS • PUBLISHER, LTD.

ISBN 978-0-398-09247-4 (paper)
ISBN 978-0-398-09248-1 (ebook)

Library of Congress Catalog Card Number: 2018038368

With THOMAS BOOKS *careful attention is given to all details of manufacturing and design. It is the Publisher's desire to present books that are satisfactory as to their physical qualities and artistic possibilities and appropriate for their particular use.* THOMAS BOOKS *will be true to those laws of quality that assure a good name and good will.*

Printed in the United States of America
MM-C-1

Library of Congress Cataloging-in-Publication Data

Names: Shaw, Elijah, author. | June, Dale L., author.
Title: An introduction to celebrity protection and touring : a guide to
　　mastering the business of VIP security / by Elijah Shaw and Dale
　　June.
Description: Springfield, Illinois : Charles C Thomas, Publisher, Ltd.,
　　[2019] | Includes index.
Identifiers: LCCN 2018038368 (print) | LCCN 2018052092 (ebook) |
　　ISBN 9780398092481 (ebook) | ISBN 9780398092474 (pbk.)
Subjects: LCSH: Bodyguards. | Celebrities—Protection. | Private security services.
Classification: LCC HV8290 (ebook) | LCC HV8290 .S485 2019
　　(print) | DDC 363.28/9—dc23
LC record available at https://lccn.loc.gov/2018038368

This book is dedicated to the next generation of protectors who have a desire to break the stereotypes of the past and advance the profession onward and upward.

—EJS

My efforts in this book are dedicated to all the fine men and women who have dedicated their lives to helping those who, for reasons beyond their control, have a need to be protected and secure in their pursuit of fame, celebrity, and riches.

—DLJ

FOREWORD

Elijah Shaw is one of the best in the business of executive protection. Throughout the years, I have had the pleasure of watching him grow his skills, his business, and his brand. He has also offered excerpts of his expertise to others by sharing his knowledge of the field through his training courses. His resume and clientele read like a who's who of your favorite A-list celebrities, so it's no surprise why he is so highly sought after.

As a 27-year music industry veteran on the business side, one constant thought resonates strongly with me every time I meet a new up-and-coming star for the first time: "I wonder if this novice entertainer will confuse employing hired muscle versus great executive protection." There is a difference. Any big man or woman with muscles can play the role of security; however, it takes a great skill set to understand human behaviors, particularly in the entertainment industry.

I first met Elijah many years ago when we represented the same client in separate capacities. I was responsible for the promotional appearances, and Elijah was responsible for the logistical elements of moving and securing the VIP. To date, Elijah's approach to safety and his attention to detail is my gold standard. By the time anyone arrives at a venue, Elijah already knows the event space layout better than anyone. He adapts quickly to any given scenario, whether working in an isolated capacity or liaising with the on-site venue staff to ensure that his standards are met. Working with him, I witnessed firsthand what professionalism and diligence to the protocol of safety and security look like.

The entertainment industry is overwhelmed with high-profile clients encountering high-risk situations. Where in the past, most of those unfortunate encounters could be kept relatively quiet, these days, many play out publicly for the amusement or derision of others via social media. Whether it is a red-carpet appearance, or merely walking out of a hotel room, the public never sees the intricacies of having to navigate some of the more nightmarish logistics. It takes a well-seasoned professional to know how to move a client through a 20,000-seat concert venue filled with screaming fans, to a 20-person intimate dinner with make-or-break executives in attendance, all under a time constraint. Yet I've seen him do both, making each transition flow seamlessly, while making himself virtually invisible—an unsung hero of sorts.

In my business, as much as you want to plan and keep everything on a schedule, the fact is, spontaneity is the variable that always plays a role, and last-minute changes continuously occur. You have to be fluid and quick-thinking to adjust to the unexpected movements of the client. As such, we are the behind-the-scenes players who have to balance meeting the needs and expectations of everyone around us. A fan wants a memorable experience, an event planner wants their event to run smoothly, a representative wants to be effective, tastemakers want access, the star wants to shine, and someone like Elijah and his team want to ensure that the trust put in them is not in vain.

I often equate the actions of professional security to a chess game with a bit more physicality; yet both are extremely cerebral, so the rules of engagement are still applicable. The goal is to protect the VIP (the King or Queen), survey the possible moves on the board, and always stay a few steps ahead of the opposition. This book is an insight into a world that the public rarely thinks of but, when executed correctly, we don't have to. Let this book serve as your guide to having discovered the world's first Bobby Fischer/Jason Bourne hybrid.

Consider yourself warned: Elijah Shaw is badass—and if your paths cross in person, I hope you are on the side of the angels, as I've seen that stark disapproving glare of his in action!

Enjoy.

Samantha "Baby Sam" Selolwane
Senior Vice President, Urban Promotion
RCA Records

ACKNOWLEDGMENTS

My thanks to my wonderful family, who have been a huge support system throughout, not just during the process of writing a book, but through my entire career. As you'll find in the subsequent pages, this industry can take its toll on family, so to my mother Hadiyah, my sons Jyhad, Eric, and Alex, thank you for continuing to motivate me to get up every morning. I would like to thank the people who gave me words of inspiration and encouragement: KEH, Shawna, Baby Sam, Adam, Gabs, Mez, JC, and M. I would like to thank my mentor, Bob Duggan, for giving me a positive blueprint to pattern myself after in this business, as well as thank my peers, Mark James, Raffaele Di Giorigio, Sam Alicea, Eric K, and Benjamin Alozie. Finally, I would like to thank my writing partner Dale June, one of my earliest inspirations, for getting involved in the industry. It was reading one of his earlier books, *Introduction to Executive Protection,* that cemented the fact that I wanted to make a career out of helping others.

—EJS

First and foremost, I want to thank Elijah Shaw for asking me to participate in writing this book. It is a great honor and compliment that I hold dear. Secondly, I want to thank my wife, Muslima and our son, Mohammed, for their encouragement and patience in allowing me the time I need to focus on something I strongly believe in. I write for the challenge, enjoyment, and to pass the lamp to another generation of protectors.

—DLJ

CONTENTS

	Page
Foreword	vii

Chapter
1. INTRODUCTION ... 3
2. IN THE BEGINNING ... 9
3. DEVELOP A NICHE ... 11
   - Think Outside the Box ... 12
   - The Secret Sauce ... 13
   - Elevator Pitch ... 14
   - What's in a Name? ... 14
4. PURPOSE AND PRINCIPLES OF PROTECTION ... 17
   - The Reason ... 17
   - Are You a Candidate? ... 18
   - Physical Characteristics ... 19
   - Mental Characteristics ... 20
   - Executive versus Celebrity ... 21
   - Corporate Protection ... 22
   - Profile of an Executive ... 23
   - Blending in ... 23
   - Business Norms and Practices ... 24
   - The Age Factor ... 25
   - Positions of Power ... 26
   - Know Your Role ... 26
   - Know the Ways, Wants, and Personality of the Celebrity ... 27
   - Operating in Their World ... 28
   - Protocol ... 29
   - Being the Shadow—Close Proximity Protection ... 30
   - Adaptability, Good Character, and Critical Thinking ... 30
   - Intangible Tools ... 31

        Imagination 31
        Perspective 32
        Observation 32
        Attitude 33
        Communication Skills 34
    Being Flexible 34
    Staying Engaged 35
    Situational Awareness 36
    Spatial Awareness 36

5. THE WORLD OF MUSIC 38
    Recording 38
    Touring 41
    Personal Appearances 43
    Photo Shoots 44
    Personal Time 45
    Working with the Entourage 45
    Coping with Long Hours 47
    Dealing with Temptations 50
    Working Away From Home 52
    Challenging Clients 52
    Morals and Ethical Dilemmas 54
    Ethical Dilemmas 55
    Giving and Receiving Gifts 56
    Music Resources 57
        Management Agencies 57
        The Record Company 59
        Publicists 60
        Industry Peers 61

6. THE WORLD OF FILM 63
    Studio Shoots 63
    Location Shoots 65
    Awards Shows 65
    Challenges 66
        Tedious Times 66
        Many Different Personalities and Bosses 66
        Long Periods Away From Family 67
        Safety and Security Compromises 69
    Film Resources 72
        The Talent Agency 73

	The Movie Studio 73
	Production Companies 73
	Practical Issues and Techniques 75
	Profile of a Celebrity 75
	Narcissism 75
	Schedules and the Celebrity Client 76
	The Celebrity Performance Schedule 77
	Instant Fame 78
	Not in the Job Description 79
	Who Gets the Coffee? 80
	Celebrity and Accessibility 81
	The Adance Survey 82
	Anticipate 82
	Plan 82
	Prepare 83
	Cloning the Protector 84
	Subtlety Wins 84
	Security Survey 85
7.	VEHICLES 87
	Advance Preparation 87
	Standards 87
	Specialty Vehicles 88
	What You Need to Learn 89
	Capacity 89
	Lighting 90
	Radio 90
	Temperature Control 90
	GPS 90
	Door Locks 91
	Seatbelts 91
	Gas Tank 91
	Tires 91
	Fire Extinguisher and Medical Kits 91
	Flairs, Reflectors, and Jumper Cables 92
	Placement 92
	Oil Stains and Being on Time 93
	Moving In and Out of Cars 93
	Doors Open 94
	The Driver's Role 94

	Embussing and Debussing	96
	Motorcades	96
	Choosing a Driver	98
	Tour Buses	99
8.	POSITIONING AND WALKING WITH CLIENTS	101
	Body Mechanics	102
	Moving the Client	103
	Preventing Problems Before They Happen	108
	Reacting to Threats	108
	Attacks on Principal (AOP)	110
	Stalking	110
	Psychological Mindfulness of Stalkers	112
	Celebrity Stalking	114
	Madonna	114
	Justin Bieber	114
	Catherine Zeta-Jones and Michael Douglas	115
	Gwyneth Paltrow	115
	Taylor Swift	115
	Why Do People Worship Celebrities?	115
	Three Levels of Celebrity Worship	116
	Entertainment-Social	116
	Intense-Personal	116
	Borderline-Pathological	116
	Fans versus Obsessive Fans	117
	Christina Grimmie Killed by Obsessed Stalker, Kevin Loibl	119
	"I Can Make You Love Me"—The Story of Laura Black	120
	Protective Intelligence and Assessment	121
9.	RED CARPET EVENTS	123
	The Red Carpet	128
	Photographers	128
	Interviews	130
	Fans	131
	Seating	134
10.	EVENT SECURITY	139
	Event Security Staff	139
	Placement	140
	Credentials: Limiting and Controlling Access	141
	Common Types of Passes	143
	FOH	143

    Escort VIP Pass Only 143
    Backstage with Escort 143
    All Access, FOH, No Escort Privileges 143
    All Access, Full Escort 144
    Press Pit Only 144
    Working Pass 144
    Stage Worker 144
  Limiting Passess 144
  Backstage Crashers 145
  The Festival Crasher 146
  Securing the Stage 148
  Signing Sessions 149
11. WORKING WITH THE MEDIA 153
  Dealing with Paparazzi and Preventing Embarrassment 153
  Press versus Paparazzi 155
12. ADDITIONAL CONSIDERATIONS 159
  Law Enforcement versus Protective Services 159
  Similarities 160
  Disengagement 160
  Power versus Force 162
  Sexual Harassment 163
13. CONCLUSION 166

APPENDIX 167
  Advance Protective Agent Checklists 167
    Things to do Before Departing for Assignment 167
    Principal 168
    Arrival at Site/City of Visit 168
  Site Surveys 169
    Types of Security Surveys 171
    Basic Perimeter Security Theory 171
    Things to Consider While Developing Plans 172
  Hotel Advance 173
    Principal's Suite 173
    Command Post 173
    Hotel Services 174
    Fire System 174
    Other Hotel Advance Considerations 174
    Hotel Advance 174

　　　　Make a Thorough Examination of the Principal's Suite 175
　　　　Meeting with Rooms Reservation Manager 175
　　　　Meeting with Assistant Manager and Security Chief 176
　　　　Command Post Equipment 177
　　Route Survey 178
　　Airport Security Surveys 179
　　Banquets, Ballrooms, and Auditoriums 180
　　Restaurants 182
　　Outdoor Events 182
　　Team Movement (On Foot or Vehicle) 183
　　Team Briefing 183
　　　　Team Leader 183
　　　　Team Briefing Format 184
　　Hospital Site Survey 185
　　　　Contacts 186
　　　　Details 186
　　　　Security 187
　　　　Police 189
　　　　Fire Department 190
　　　　Emergency Room 191
　　　　Parking Areas 192
　　　　Perimeter of Hospital (Interior-Exterior) 193
　　　　Overall Security and Disaster Preparedness 193
　　　　Employees 194

Index 197

AN INTRODUCTION TO CELEBRITY PROTECTION AND TOURING

Chapter 1

INTRODUCTION

Elijah J. Shaw, July 2018
Dale L. June, July 2018

For close to three decades now, I've been working with celebrities, high net-worth individuals, and VIPs to protect them from both harm and embarrassment. In this book, I want to give readers a sense of what this profession is really all about, separating fact from fantasy, and emphasizing the real world over the textbook. As an instructor, these philosophies are incorporated into the lessons that I teach, when my schedule permits, at the ICON Training Academy. The courses, like the business itself, are rewarding on multiple levels, and the challenge is how to fit all my passions and pursuits into an extremely hectic operational schedule. This dilemma has plagued me over the years: how do I create the time to educate individuals in the industry and on the industry, when time is the one thing I have so very little of? The solution to this problem you now hold in your hands in the form of this book.

The book is designed for a wide readership, from those brand-new to the profession, who are in the process of deciding if this is the career for them, to individuals with various degrees of experience in the business, who stay sharp by continuously adding updated tools to their toolkit.

As I see it, no matter the specific area an individual is working in (or plans to work in), be it with corporations, celebrities, the clergy, or politicians, the basic building blocks are the same: we provide personal (close) protection to our clients, with them becoming our protectees. However, this is much more than just physical protection—providing a body to guard a body. We are more than that, and as such, must reevaluate regularly, for just as the threats have evolved, so must we.

That means giving increased attention to critical thinking, logistical planning, and sound problem-solving, and when applied correctly, we find that this has the amazing benefit of reducing or eliminating the need to ever get physical in the first place. The ability to do all of that, as well as to be ready to respond effectively if the need does arise, is what separates the trained from the untrained.

However, just as there are similarities, there are also differences inherent with the specific type of protectee you're working with. Celebrities often have a need for our services, not just because of the bad guys, but also because of their fans, ranging from the well-intentioned to the obsessive. This type of protective posture and response is different from other categories of high net-worth individuals, who while wealthy, don't have the spotlight on them in terms of public adoration and the dark side that potentially comes with it. Consider a corporate executive who, while facing a degree of potential risk, has different challenges. The routine of protecting him from his home to his office and back is a very different story from being stage-left with an entertainer who's performing in front of 20,000 screaming fans.

Even the pace of celebrity protection is unique, due to the ebb and flow of the assignments and situations you can be in. These can range from being so active that you feel you need to clone yourself just to get everything done, to waiting for hours on end for the client to come out of his or her dressing room. Adjusting to this dynamic is difficult for some and impossible for others. Many get into celebrity protection not realizing the scope of their duties or the totality of the client's dependence on the service, and they can feel like they are adrift at sea.

However, I don't want to paint the impression that you will always be going it alone. There are times when you will be working with a team of individuals, like-minded or otherwise, and even as a solo operator your thought process and outlook must still reflect a team mentality as you interact with the protectee, with their staff, with law enforcement, with the press, and with the fans. These are all members of the team, and it will be up to you to make sure they play ball like national champions instead of butting heads and imploding like children on the playground.

It's still weird for me to think that, since college, this has been the only industry I've ever worked in (minus that one-year stint selling cars, but that's a story for another book). I'll humbly go on record to state that I've found this career to be a blessing for me on multiple levels and for a variety of reasons. For example, due to the nature of my profession, a kid who grew up in a housing project on the south side of Chicago well under the poverty line has been able to see the world, literally, a few times over. Those work trips have ignited a personal passion for international travel (and a collection of frequent flyer miles). So far, I've travelled to 73 countries and six of the seven continents. The profession gives me not just a living, but long-term financial independence.

However, most importantly, it has given me a chance to grow as a human being, learning about myself as I've learned about the people I've worked with. I've also been able to pay it forward by being in a position to be able to give back to the community. I've done this by offering *pro bono* protection for women who have been victims of domestic abuse and for the shelters that support them. Additionally, for several years now, I've offered merit-based scholarships to the ICON Training Academy directed at individuals who want the training, but much like me at the beginning of my career, financially might not have the means. Now with this latest endeavor at finally tackling authorship (thanks, Mark!), I hope that pulling these concepts, philosophies, and tactics out of my head and putting them on paper will be helpful as our industry, like the rest of the world, evolves.

> The great successful men of the world have used their imagination; they think ahead and create their mental picture in all its details, filling in here, adding a little there, altering this a bit and that a bit, but steadily building—steadily building.
> —Robert Collier[1]

To be rich and famous is the dream of young artists, musicians and actors, despite the fact that it's a long hard road and only a chosen few finally make it to the top where they can say they have arrived. One famous comedian of the 1990s said he knew he was successful when he could write a check for a million dollars. That was his personal measurement of success, while others invest in art or large homes in

---

1. Retrieved 11/12/17 from motivatingquotes.com/achievement.htm.

Malibu near the ocean. They have large social media followings and adoring fans, and everywhere they go they are given the royal treatment benefitting their star celebrity status.

Yet, as celebrity grows, so grows the amount of trials and complications. What started as a single companion now balloons to an entourage that contains advisors, handlers, promoters, fixers and hangers-on. Then there are the ever-present *paparazzi*[2] pushing and shoving, vying for the best position to gain the most advantageous spot to document every movement of the celebrity. The overly enthusiastic photographer will even stake out and stalk the object of his professional attention, popping up here, appearing there, springing out of nowhere, causing surprise and even fear in the celebrity.

Adding to the complexity of the celebrity's life are the ever-present and all-seeing eyes and presence of the protectors who become a necessary, perhaps stabilizing element between the celebrity and the chaos of their life. Yet as necessary as they are, the protectors may not always be appreciated.

> I couldn't go anywhere unless there was a security guard with me. That spoiled my life. It was like being in captivity. Those days are gone, and I don't ever want to see that happen to me again. Now I can wander around the streets of Los Angeles on my own. I like it that way.
> —Christine McVie, Member of Fleetwood Mac[3]

Fame equals fans: fans by the thousands, adoring, admiring, affectionate. They form a type of symbiotic relationship with the entertainer; they buy the music, appreciate the art, and attend the concerts. All they want is to be a part of the artist's world, even if only for a short time. They are the ordinary fans who like what they see and hear and, though enthusiastic, will remain relatively considerate of the performer and their personal life.

---

2. Paparazzi are independent photographers who take pictures of high-profile people such as athletes, entertainers, politicians, and other celebrities, typically while the subjects go about their usual life routines. Paparazzi tend to make a living by selling their photographs to media outlets focusing on tabloid journalism and sensationalism. In his book, *Word and Phrase Origins,* author Robert Hendrickson writes that Federico Fellini's 1959 film, *La Dolce Vita,* took the name *paparazzi* from an Italian dialect word for a particularly noisy, buzzing mosquito. Retrieved 12/18/17 from paparazzicelebrity.blogspot.com/2007/03/history-of-paparazzi.html
3. Quoted in June, Dale L. (2016). *Introduction to Executive Protection* (3rd ed.). Boca Raton: CRC Press.

Like all other aspects of life, there are also those whose interest goes way beyond mere appreciation. They are the ones who imagine the actor is in love with them, or they feel that they have been singled out as special and are entitled to privileges such as access to backstage and other events that a normal fan would be excluded from. When that fan is rebuffed or doesn't feel they are receiving the attention they desire, there is a very thin line between love and hate. They become a nuisance, a stalker, or perhaps even a potential killer. That is the expensive part of the price of fame.

There are a number of celebrities who have been threatened, stalked, and even murdered by fans. Most of these incidents could have been prevented or mitigated with adequately trained and experienced security. Our hope is that a book such as this provides many answers to offset the lack of knowledge and protocols for providing exceptional services to mega-entertainers as well as up-and-coming talent.

"With Love, Rebecca," is how model and actress Rebecca Schaffer, then an up-and-coming star of the 1980s sit-com *My Sister, Sam* signed a photograph requested by an obsessed fan, Robert John Bardo. That autograph began three years of stalking and terror, eventually leading to the shooting death of twenty-one-year-old Schaffer by Bardo.

The Bardo-Schaffer attack eventually led the governor of California to sign legislation prohibiting the Department of Motor Vehicles from providing home addresses of California's drivers to the public. Bardo paid a private investigator $240 to obtain a copy of Schaffer's driver license with her home address. This action created one of the major ripples that led to the security subset we now term *celebrity protection*.

What is the difference between VIP (high-risk executive and political personnel) protection and celebrity protection? What is the difference between a bodyguard and an executive protection specialist? Aren't they all the same? The answer is Yes, and No. This book explores the similarities and differences with a fine focus on celebrity protection in the worlds of entertainment, sports, and film.

Several books and articles have been written about close personal protection, also known as executive protection, including *Introduction to Executive Protection* (D. June, CRC Press, 2015), but nothing before this book has specifically addressed celebrity security to this depth. The purpose of this book is to specialize in the narrow, yet forever expanding, niche of providing full-range security to high public profile figures who, for whatever reason, have security requirements.

This book, addressing everything from threat and safety assessments to award shows and touring security problems, will be beneficial to celebrities, their entourage, and others charged with safeguarding their interests. Additionally, we hope it will become a well-referred handbook to the professionals who stand between a celebrity and any potential harmful or embarrassing act against the person in the public eye.

With that said, the reader of this book will not have to be an established professional security expert to benefit from it. It is written in layman's language, easily understood by the security novice as well as the casual reader.

> . . . The moment we become conscious of what we are, then we become responsible for everything we are and do.
> —James Christian in The Art of Wondering[4]

---

4. Quote appearing in Jones, John R. and Carlson, Daniel P. (2004). *Reputable Conduct* (2nd ed.). Upper Saddle River NJ: Pearson/Prentice-Hall, p. 35.

Chapter 2

IN THE BEGINNING

The job of the bodyguard has a very long history going back to the very earliest of civilizations, including Egyptian, Roman, and Greek times. The term has been constant through all cultures and has seen many evolutions, from the elite martial units of kings and emperors to bullet blockers for gangland thugs, to highly trained and sophisticated licensed professionals.

In reality, the term *executive protection* is a bit misleading for high-level security services based off of its origins. It began in the early 1970s when President Nixon established the Executive Protection Service in government. The role was for uniformed officers to be assigned to protect embassies and high-ranking diplomats. The name caught on in private security circles and eventually has been co-opted to describe protective services for politicians, VIPs, heads of state, royalty, wealthy clients, and celebrities who for whatever reason feel a need to have security close to them.

In the late 1990s, executive protection became a familiar corporate word and the catch-all phrase describing risk management, deterrence, and out-of-uniform security. The idea of executive protection (close personal protection) includes all the principles of protection, such as determination of actual and potential vulnerabilities, careful analysis and planning, preparation, implementation of a well-conceived plan, advance security arrangements, and the total awareness to provide a safe and secure environment. In the broader sense, close personal protection is a security program designed around the lifestyle, family, and environment of the individual being protected. It means anticipating, preparing and planning for any contingency that would place the person being protected in a vulnerable or life-threatening position.[1] The goal in close personal protection is to proactively prevent incidents from ever occurring and, failing that, to shield or remove one's client from harm's way.

---

1. Quoted in June, Dale L. (2016). *Introduction to Executive Protection* (3rd ed.). Boca Raton: CRC Press.

Chapter 3

DEVELOP A NICHE

Celebrity protection is in some ways a unique market. But in marketing, the more specific you can be, the more successful you will be in finding customers. This means that it's helpful, sometimes necessary, to research, develop, and define a niche, carving out a select piece of a bigger industry to specialize in.

Consider that when a client has to select someone to go on an assignment, if most bodyguards offer (on the surface) similar services, how do you distinguish yourself from the pack? That is where niche marketing comes in.

Rest assured that having a niche does not mean that is the only thing you do. My niche is celebrity protection. Having done it for close to three decades, it is what I am most recognized for in the business, in much the way my co-author is best known for his time having served with the United States Secret Service under multiple administrations. Yet celebrity protection is not the only thing I do; in fact, not by a longshot. My roster of clients includes everything from historic high net-worth families, to corporate executives at Fortune 500 companies, to politicians on both sides of the aisle. I've provided close protection for noncelebrity VIPs, having taken them as far as the Great Wall of China and to the back streets of Palestine. In fact, as of this writing, I'm beginning the initial preplanning stages of providing protective services related to the 2020 Republican and Democratic National Conventions. I currently have six of those political conventions under my belt.

Still, what I am best known for is working with celebrities, and I am okay with that. Throughout the years, I have developed and cultivated the image so that when somebody needs celebrity protection services, they think of Elijah Shaw. It's not to the exclusion of the other slices of the protection pie (corporate, religious, high risk PSD), but it helps from a branding perspective.

As you read this book, think about your own niche. Think about what you can do to distinguish yourself from the pack. For example, do you speak a second language? All else being equal, a potential client who is going to spend three months in Spain filming a movie is much more likely to select an agent who is fluent in Spanish, as they'll be able to speak and listen to the locals.

However, remember, even if you have something that distinguishes you from the pack, you have to figure out how to convey that information to the decision-makers, as those are the people who will recommend or hire you. Once you define your niche, make sure you communicate it clearly to those who may have a need.

If you speak Spanish, mention that on your website, your business card, and anything else that interfaces with the potential decision-makers. Let them know that you are a multilingual Spanish-speaking executive protection agent, so when someone is looking for an agent to go into Latin America, you can make it easier for them to find you.

THINK OUTSIDE THE BOX

I once had a student in one of my courses who, size-wise, would be considered of a smaller stature. While he did extremely well in the course, there was a noticeable height difference between him and the majority of the other agents. During a periodic follow-up call after the course, he said, "You know, Elijah, I'm having the hardest time here. I just can't figure out how to get the traction I need to really break through into the industry. I work assignments here and there, and then the phone goes quiet. I think it may be because of my build. It's kind of hitting at my self-confidence, and I don't know what to do."

Understanding his dilemma, we took it back to the basics. I asked him, "What is something that you would consider unique that you're good at doing?" I was really trying to help him visualize and develop his niche. I kept bringing up examples, and at one point, I said, "Just think, what if you knew sign language? I would imagine that in the wide world of high net-worth individuals, there have to be more than one or two who are hearing-impaired or may have children who are hearing-impaired. If you knew sign language, can you see how that might give you the advantage over other protectors, all else being equal?"

He got really quiet on the phone, and then he said, "Elijah, my mother was born deaf." Turned out that he was fluent in sign language, having been raised in a household where it was used regularly. I could practically see the light bulb go on in his head and the gears start turning.

For him, his marketing plan would then go on to include identifying high net-worth individuals who were hearing impaired, or with an immediate family member in that category. I also had him research associations that advocate for the deaf, supposing that if one of their wealthy donors had to pick him or a different, nonsign language speaking agent for an assignment, say a mission trip to a riskier part of the world, he would have a clear advantage.

Your niche can be built around something that you do better than others, a unique skill that might even seem, on the surface, unrelated to close protection. Perhaps you are a long-distance runner. I remember reading of Anil Ambani, the billionaire who runs marathons. You can imagine that if a position opened on his security detail, they might give some additional consideration to an agent who had several marathons under his or her belt.

About a year ago, I received a call from someone looking for a protector. They wanted an agent who was qualified for scuba, as the client was going to Miami and planned to do some diving while there. I recommended a former student who did scuba, and upon completion of what was thought to be a one-off assignment, that agent has gone on to work with that client on many different occasions. He has also kept earning additional scuba certifications and has established a foothold in that space. The niche, as distinct as it was, was his entry into a long working relationship with that client and others.

THE SECRET SAUCE

Not everyone who reads this will act on the tips and strategies provided within these pages. In the same vein, not everyone who works with a client once or twice, only to have the phone go quiet for weeks on end, will stick with it. When it comes to client development, this isn't a business of immediate results. However, those who keep at it, combining skill and tenacity, can have a wonderful long-term career.

Remember, this is the protection *business,* and as such, you have to treat it like a business. What every business has to do is continue to identify new clients and keep their existing clients happy in order to continue working. Don't just think about how you can get more clients. Think about what you need to do to keep the ones you have. There aren't many shortcuts in life, and the same goes for developing the brand of YOU.

ELEVATOR PITCH

As part of the marketing development of the brand of YOU, you need to develop an elevator pitch. That's the 30-second version of who you are and what you do. Even if you never deliver it to anyone in an actual elevator, creating one is a good exercise, because it forces you to define and communicate your niche in only a few words.

You need to condense whatever you do so that it's short and simple. It might be, "I'm a licensed bodyguard and a former police detective." That tells me that you've got credentials and the experience in just a few words. Take the time to figure out not just what your niche is, but what that niche means to a potential client. Focus on the benefit to them more than on the details of what you do and how you do it. Practice and tailor your delivery so that you can paint a picture succinctly.

WHAT'S IN A NAME?

In the book and movie, *The Godfather,* the character Luca Brasi is one of Don Vito Corleone's personal enforcers. Brasi is portrayed as slow-witted and brutish, but his ruthlessness and his fierce loyalty to Don Corleone mean he is both feared and respected. Brasi is portrayed as the stereotypical bodyguard so often seen in movies and novels. He is a hulking individual lurking in the shadow of the person he is hired to protect from all physical menaces. He reacts to threats with violence and strength, not really an image that the profession wants to be known for these days. Remember this, as we will come back to it shortly.

Now let's do a quick exercise: what does your business card say? If you don't yet have one, that's fine, but before you read any further, visualize what your title would be. Does it say, Executive Protection Agent? Personal Protection Specialist? Certified Protection Specialist? Licensed Private Investigator? Licensed Security Officer? Private Investigator?

What you put on your card, like what you put on your website or social media page, is what the potential client takes away from the interaction. Like all marketing, it should be about what the client needs, and in this case that means speaking the language of your audience.

What you will notice is that throughout this book, unlike many in the industry, I do not shy away from the term *bodyguard*. Say that word, and the picture that often would come to mind is the stereotypical bruiser or knuckle-dragger mentioned above, and modern protectors do not want to be associated with that type of image. Instead, they choose many of the other terms I offered in an effort to present a more professional description of what we do. While this is a very noble sentiment and I support it, there is one problem with that particular line of thinking:

Most clients don't know what any of those words really mean.

Just try and explain what a "Level 3A Close Protection Operative" is in a 30-second elevator pitch. It's pretty tough. Even if you somehow have a few minutes, you might see the potential client's eyes start glazing over as they tune out. That's because you would be speaking our language and not their language, and that's not what successful marketing is about.

Here's a rough and dirty example. Log onto your computer and type the words, "Executive Protection Specialist" in the search tab. Take a look at the number of relevant results that search brings back. Then do a new search, typing in the word "bodyguard." You will find that (at least at the time of this writing) almost twice as many people use the latter, which gives it more relevance. So, from a pure marketing perspective, even if it's strictly web-based, I'm going to want to use the word, "bodyguard," in my lexicon because the general public knows what that is.

If I were discussing film with a movie director, I could talk about the Best Boy and the Key Grip. But if I were to have that same conversation with a person who simply loves watching movies, they would look at me in confusion, because those are terms specific to the film industry. Understanding this, you can tailor your message for your audience. Take business cards: these days, you can get a nice set of cards for as low as $25. What that means is that you can get *two* nice sets of business cards for $50. I say that because you then would have two different ways of tailoring your message. I have multiple sets of cards: for the layperson, my title reads, "Bodyguard"; for professionals in the industry, I present the other card, which lists me as a "Security Consultant."

Try and figure out how to incorporate your niches into your marketing plans. You will have a lot of competition when someone searches "bodyguard," on the web, but if you include on your website that you have Spanish-speaking bodyguards, that's going to narrow down the results pool dramatically so that customers looking for that needle can find you in the haystack. My philosophy is to reclaim the name, so that when they hear it they won't think of *The Godfather,* but rather be impressed with your actions and professionalism.

Chapter 4

PURPOSE AND PRINCIPLES OF PROTECTION

> I don't want expensive gifts; I don't want to be bought. I have everything I want. I just want someone to be there for me, to make me feel safe and secure.[1]
>
> —Diana, Princess of Wales

THE REASON

The purpose of personal protection is to provide a safe, secure environment for those who are rich, famous, or influential to a segment of society. Correspondingly, persons in need of protective services hire others to build a safe, secure environment around them based on explicit but simple security principles.

1. Protection must be layered.
2. Protectors must be constantly alert of protectee positioning in regards to the environment.
3. Visual awareness—seeing peripherally in conjunction with centered vision.
4. Not leaving an assigned post until properly relieved.
5. Constant security state of mind.
6. Constant communication and teamwork (the person being protected included).
7. Challenge all unauthorized persons in the vicinity.
8. Investigate unusual activities and suspicious packages and objects.
9. Assertively being proactive and cautious.
10. Knowledgeable of procedures, processes, and personnel.

---
1. Retrieved February 12, 2018; https://www.brainyquote.com/quotes/princess_diana_154338

ARE YOU A CANDIDATE?

Like any specialization, hiring requirements vary, but most agencies are looking for fair-minded, effective, and resourceful individuals. Many firms make sure they carefully screen potential agents on the basis of the skills they bring to the table combined with their personality traits and achievements.

Amongst the important selection criteria are:

- Background should be void of felony crimes (sex-related, major theft, child and spousal abuse). Background should reflect positive responsibility.
- Financial responsibility is considered, so as to not be tempted into theft.
- Good psychological well-being, good mental health and maturity. These criteria can indicate good judgment, critical thinking, decision-making and management of stress.
- Communication, writing and interpersonal skills are considered.
- Physically able to take on the demands of the career. A physical fitness, self-defense, and nutritional regimen can lessen physical stress, provide confidence, increase longevity, and reduce the potential for injury.
- Any form of education shows commitment. Higher education and specialized Executive Protection courses are particularly noticed.
- A Military and/or law enforcement background is an excellent entryway into the business in many employers' eyes.

A few characteristics a bodyguard should possess are:

- The ability to assume leadership and responsibility.
- Able to take on various types of situations and assignments.
- Apply critical thinking[2] while displaying maturity and professionalism.

---

2. Critical thinking is analysis. It is the ability for a person to think for themselves as an individual. To be a critical thinker, a person must be willing to look deeper into a subject than what is obvious. It may require research, study, and pondering of a topic to understand its full depth. Critical thinkers do not necessarily stop at what is simple or obvious; they look for alternatives and possibilities outside of what they initially encounter. Critical thinking skills include the ability to challenge common assumptions by formulating questions, identifying and weighing appropriate evidence, and reaching reasoned conclusions. It is a synonym for ensuring that you account for all significant consequences by developing the habit of using your imagination. In a word, critical thinking is analysis.

- A display of leadership skills, open-mindedness, and fairness needed to manage situations.
- Empathy: being able to emotionally relate to the insecurity and fears of the person being protected.
- Trustworthiness is needed for both fellow protectors and the person being protected. They must be able to be counted on to perform their duty.
- Integrity, Intelligence, Interpersonal Skills and Imagination.
- A good knowledge of emergency medical treatment (training as an emergency medical technician is highly recommended).
- Ability to remain calm in times of quickly escalating and changing circumstances.

Today's protective operator must be skilled in numerous areas such as sociology, psychology, human relations, and much more. He or she is a coach, an ambassador representing the client, a psychologist, a guide, a counselor, and the person to call when help is needed.

Protectors tend to be Type A personalities who are competitive, driven and, at times, impatient. They may also exhibit obsessive-compulsive behaviors, which in turn has the effect of making them good at aspects of the job: by checking and rechecking, no detail is too small to overlook.

Each person has his own reason, his own motivations to enter this field. It may be the prestige, the power, the opportunity for travel to places some can only imagine, the privilege of walking among presidents, royalty, and titans of industry and finance. It could be the money: the occupation does pay well, though anyone who places money as a major motivation might invite closer scrutiny.

In the final analysis, there is only one primary reason: individuals come into this business because they plan to be dedicated to the craft. Those who make a lasting career out of this profession have a sincere drive, perhaps even a compulsive desire, to help those who have a need.

PHYSICAL CHARACTERISTICS

Physical characteristics of the protector may vary depending on the perspectives and requirements of the client. For some, the requirement will be for a person who blends easily into the crowd and staff surrounding the client; for others, it can be just the opposite as they want them to stand out. Average height and weight, appropriately dressed and groomed, physically fit with stamina to endure long hours, and strength to able to restrain overzealous fans and counter any threats are common parameters. In some instances, the protectors physically dwarf the client on an extreme scale. For example, professional boxing champion Floyd Mayweather, all of 5'8" and 150 pounds, has bodyguards of the following proportions: 7'1" and 430 pounds; 6'7" and 380 pounds; 6'5" and 400 pounds; and 6'3" and 260 pounds.

While some may ridicule, as the client, Mayweather is entitled to request whatever he wants in the form of a protector. In this case, his requirements for size and weight of his protector are more of an anomaly than the average agent in the marketplace. However, a deeper dive would take into consideration how much of a showman this particular VIP is, and how that may have factored into his staffing decisions. While extreme, we use this as an example to state that protectors indeed come in all shapes, sizes, and genders.

MENTAL CHARACTERISTICS

Mentally and emotionally having the ability to quickly assess an evolving problem and make a correct diagnosis and solution is imperative. Mental fitness and emotional strength define the attitude and psychological personality of the protector. Often the long hours without an opportunity to sleep or eat and extensive travel take a huge toll on our mental welfare and mindset. In some cases, the glamour of the profession can be addictive: the thrill of the fast life, from first class travel and accommodations to having the opportunity to rub shoulders with personalities you've only seen on the big screen, can be like dopamine to the brain.

Like a drug, the protection of celebrities can bring euphoric highs and dark negative lows in some. Over time, the lows can begin to take higher and higher priced tolls. Like similar professions offering degrees of potential danger, we encounter phases very similar to law enforcement, military, and other first responders, whose stress levels are elevated for extended periods.

In phase one, an agent may be considered awestruck and enthusiastic. This can be referred to as the honeymoon phase. The agent is enthusiastic, and fully absorbed in the work. Their attitude is gung ho and idealistic, and they are often the subject of conversations by friends and family telling them how lucky they are to be in that privileged position. The money is good, and ancillary benefits make them feel as if they are living a life on par with the client.

In phase two, the enthusiasm has dwindled and the excitement dampened. The daily activities have become more routine, and things that were exciting previously are now much more commonplace and mundane. This phase is referred to as settling down. Stress of travel, being away from home and family for long periods of time, missing holidays, vacations, and family activities can weigh heavily, so much so that the protector might even become lethargic and depressed.

During phase three, the protector is dealing with disillusionment, becoming cynical, distrusting, and pessimistic. They feel unappreciated and begin regretting not living a normal life with family and friends. Work becomes a means to a paycheck, and temptations receive more consideration as the agent might view them as entitlements for all he has given, and given up, since the assignment began.

Phase four brings an agent to the crossroads. By this time, he realizes he has invested too much time to the job, and he is nearing or has reached an age where he realizes his body can no longer endure the physical and mental stress. He senses that he has made many selfish sacrifices for his occupation over the concerns and needs of his family. Some will let this mode of thinking defeat them, leaving them disgruntled and bitter, while others will use this as a moment of transformation, perhaps transitioning into supervisory roles or moving into ancillary roles such as teaching or mentorship.

The career survivors in this field are those who are self-aware enough to see and navigate around the pitfalls. Their adaptability will allow them to not only survive but thrive in a demanding segment of the industry.

EXECUTIVE VERSUS CELEBRITY

At first glance, executive and celebrity protection look pretty much alike. The concepts of establishing a safe, secure environment, threat assessment, route planning, and static positioning are all core concepts. There is one main underlining code, and that is to be sure that the person being protected (the protectee) suffers no harm or embarrassment through the intentional or unintentional actions of an assailant.

However, with the rise of new media stoking fandom and the professionalization of the paparazzi into a hungry and aggressive business model, specialists in celebrity protection have forged an ongoing evolution in traditional close personal protection, adapting to the new landscape on behalf of their clients. A basic executive protection program is concerned with providing security at the protectee's home, business, and travel, where the normal routine is essentially the same, regardless of the setting. Celebrity protection differs, because the work environment comes in a near infinite variety of circumstances and locations, from overcrowded stadiums to private white sandy beaches. The appearance of a highly famous person from the stage, screen, television, or sports will draw huge crowds of spectators, and the possibility exists that not all of them will be adoring fans. The ability to understand the totality of the craft is therefore important on multiple levels.

CORPORATE PROTECTION

While the focus of this book is celebrity protection, I think it's appropriate to begin with a brief overview of the most mainstream slice of the pie, namely corporate protection, aka the protection of executives in the traditional business mold. I suppose if we are comparing apples to apples, it wouldn't be considered the most glamorous part of the industry; however, in my opinion, it is the most stable. In corporate protection, you may not find yourself moving your protectee to and from the stage, movie set, or recording studio, yet you will be much more likely to benefit from some of the most consistent long-term work in the marketplace.

In executive protection, the expectation is often for security people to do their jobs and remain unseen. Remember, your client has a level of standing within the company, and how he or she is viewed by others is important. The challenge is often how do you blend into that corporate culture? Simultaneously, how do you position yourself so that you can be effective enough to defeat an adversary (or more importantly, prevent an incident from happening in the first place), but not stand out so that the client feels that he or she has a babysitter? Corporate executives are Alpha personalities, and no Alpha personality wants to have someone looking over his shoulder all the time by choice. You as the protector must figure out a way to do your job while giving the clients the space they need to do theirs.

If you maintain an overtly visible presence, you run the risk of making your client look weak to their peers, competitors, and subordinates. Therefore, one of the goals is to be able to exist in the vicinity of the client, allowing you to be effective without being overbearing. One of the more favorable techniques for countering this challenge is the use of *zero presence:* in essence, being able to conduct protective services to benefit the VIP without the world, or at times even the protectee, even being aware of you or your team's presence in the vicinity.

PROFILE OF AN EXECUTIVE

Most executives are self-made. While some may have been born into wealth, having inherited the companies they run, a vast majority have worked themselves up the ranks in the highly competitive world of business and have the bona fides to show for it. They've reached their positions and their wealth by focusing on their goals and working tirelessly to reach them. That also means that their expectation is for you to do the same—without getting in their way as they work their magic.

BLENDING IN

The corporation has existed long before your date of hire, and each company has a specific way of doing things. This way of doing things is the company's corporate culture, and as a protector, it is your job to blend into said culture in such a way that you do not become an eyesore or an interference. One way to accomplish that is by dressing the part. If your client wears a business suit, then you more often than not will need to wear a business suit. One exception to this rule is the growing number of high-tech industries where casual dress is the norm from the top down.

A word about accessories in the corporate environment: less is more. For men, no matter what your personal style is when you're off the clock, it's a good idea to leave the earrings and necklaces at home. They may help define you as an individual, but in the business world, the culture seeks to have their employees speak with one voice. Think symphony instead of guitar solo.

But it's not only about dress. You also have to speak the language of corporate executives, becoming a reflection in a sense. Model yourself the way they do as you accompany them to meetings and corporate functions. Manners also come into play: A good rule of thumb is, unless explicitly told to, you don't call the client by his first name just because you know it. Take active steps to minimize the familiarity. When accompanying the client to meetings or professional gatherings, you have to master the art of blending into the woodwork. With practice and confidence, in time you will be as familiar to the environment as the conference table, effectively hiding in plain sight.

Depending on the environment, you may even have a space of your own near your protectee's office, and while that's much nicer than having to sit in the lobby or the car all day, remember that even though the people who work with your client may know you and your role, the same may not be true for the entire company, not to mention its customers or investors. When those individuals visit the office and walk past your desk, a photo of your kids blends in a lot better than a framed picture of you shooting an AK-47 at the tactical range.

BUSINESS NORMS AND PRACTICES

By and large, the vast majority of bodyguards aren't usually drawn from the ranks of former corporate executives; therefore, you must cultivate an understanding of general business norms and practices on your own. Time is money, and you can't expect your client to train you in this. You either come in knowing it or you pick up on it quickly.

Most companies expect their employees to *work* when they're at work, and certainly this is true in the executive suite. No feet on the desk, no reading the newspaper, no personal calls (unless you have an enclosed space like an office and your client doesn't object).

Find out how they answer the phone at the company, and mirror that when you're there. Find out what the expectations are regarding food, breaks, and chatting with the people who work there; it may be appropriate to engage in polite conversation but not more than that, as familiarity might open you up to increased attention and scrutiny.

If you are expected to communicate in the client organization's email system, pay attention to your grammar. You don't have to try to win the Nobel prize in literature, but you should try to match the expected level of written communication.

THE AGE FACTOR

Executives don't have to project youth in the same way that music or movie stars do, and depending on the corporate culture, a youthful-looking bodyguard may actually look out of place next to a 60-year-old executive. Since executives want to project a certain professional image, they often prefer a more seasoned agent as their bodyguard, someone who fits in both in their business and social circles. They might prefer someone older simply for the times during travel when you'll be the only one to talk to. Another reality is, there are businessmen who might not take kindly to having a fit, younger man around their spouse. The Alpha Male is territorial by nature, and if the client thinks you have eyes on his better half, or even worse, that she has eyes for you, it could mean the end of your working relationship. Better, they think, to solve this problem before it starts by hiring agents outside of that demographic.

With that said, if you are on the more youthful end of the spectrum, and your interest is corporate protection, the door is not closed for you. Instead you might want to direct your energies to newer companies, particularly in the tech sector, such as Facebook, Snapchat, and Twitter, as executives there are trending younger.

Visualize what the Secret Service agents protecting the President out in public look like. Regardless of the actual age of the Commander in Chief, they all look like they belong because they do such a masterful job of blending in. Corporate protection agents also need to blend in, so no matter what your biological age is, projecting composure and maturity should be the order of the day.

POSITIONS OF POWER

Executives are used to being very much in charge, and even if they are not at the pinnacle of that particular company's corporate ladder, the fact that they would even have a need for protection means they likely are in a position of power. In many cases, they are expected to make decisions that can and do affect the livelihood of hundreds or even thousands of employees, and potentially even millions of customers. They are well-paid to make important choices daily, and they are used to the idea that, as the decision-makers, they have the final say when dealing with subordinates.

What all this means for you is that they are not going to take kindly to you telling them what to do and how to do it. Yet, at times, due to the nature of the profession, that is exactly what you will have to do. However, make no mistake: in executive protection, the client is, literally, the boss. There may well be times when you will make your case as best as you can, but have to deal with the hand you are given if the client overrules you.

KNOW YOUR ROLE

More than in other parts of the protection industry, in the corporate environment, you will be expected to quietly do your job, remaining unseen and out of the way as much as possible. The big picture is that your client would like to go about his day without interference or interruption, and your job is to make sure that he gets to do that, safely and securely.

As a rule of thumb, you'll have much less input with a corporate protectee than you will with a celebrity client. With executives, you're going to spend a lot of time at the door, a lot of time with the car, a lot of time outside of the boardroom or in the hotel lobby. Your duties may be narrower in scope, because executives have other advisors and handlers who are filling these roles that, at times, have to be assumed over on the celebrity side. The experienced business executive often knows not to ask you to do duties far outside of your job description, because they usually have a good understanding of business norms and practices. He doesn't want a call from Legal or the HR department for any violations of employment law or otherwise.

On the celebrity side, that understanding of business norms and practices doesn't necessarily exist. The reality is, a celebrity client might be only a few months removed from high school, having previously been working at McDonald's and living in their mother's basement. However, now by virtue of a hit record or athletic scholarship, they are now a multimillion-dollar commodity with a degree of exposure that needs to be protected. That individual doesn't understand business norms the way executives do. With that in mind, be aware of the differences, and decide carefully which niche you want to pursue.

KNOW THE WAYS, WANTS, AND PERSONALITY OF THE CELEBRITY

Knowing the ways, wants and personality of the client is one of the primary and potentially most challenging rules of celebrity protection. Working with a protectee is a lot like a marriage, the better you understand the person, the smoother the relationship. In a total protective environment, the protective agent begins the day with the principal in the morning, takes them to work, returns them home during the evening, and watches over their household during the night. In fact, the protective agent may spend more time with the protective assignment than with his/her own spouse and family. Getting to know the work and family environment of the protectee is as important as knowing the threat level of potential harm. It is easier to understand, anticipate, and neutralize the threat if there are as few unknowns as possible; and it is to your advantage if the business and family protective shield is also in place and enforced. If the protectee's concerns and needs are known and can be anticipated, the association will be mutually rewarding across the board.

When first introduced to the client, it is incumbent upon the protective agent to ascertain as much information about the protectee as possible. The client himself/herself will often provide a good deal of information or she may designate a staff member as primary contact for whatever additional information is necessary. It is important to get a sense of their schedule, the location of regular appointments, the names of staff and family, contact telephone numbers (24 hours a day) any known medical problems, allergies, or disabilities. In the event of medical emergency, the protectee's blood type should be known, especially if it is of a rare type. A protector does not have to be an emergency medical technician, but he should be able to identify a heart attack, heat stroke, choking, and other emergencies and have a working knowledge of CPR, plus certification in basic first aid.

Consider all personality traits of the protectee: Are they abrasive? Combative? Timid? Do they have a tendency to attract trouble? A protectee with an oversized ego may invite trouble from outsiders or they may challenge the judgment of the protection agent, resulting in head butting. This creates a situation of being a part of an assignment from hell, one in which no one wins. Strong beliefs, opinions, or convictions can also lead to problems, so be careful of what you share or chime in on. Remember, it is not necessary to like the protectee to work together efficiently. What is necessary is to remember that you have a responsibility to provide the very best good faith security effort to the protectee.[3]

OPERATING IN THEIR WORLD

By definition, a protector must be close to the person he is protecting. This places him in circumstances and positions he may never otherwise have an opportunity to be in. It is a world of high finance, exotic vacations, exclusive nightclubs, luxury cars, beautiful people, expensive clothes, personal assistants, five-star hotels, and adoring fans. In essence, it is a lifestyle foreign to the average protector except on television. His real-life world consists of car and mortgage payments, yard work, and taking the dog to the vet. He must remember when he is on duty with his protective charge that he is in their world, but not a part of it. When his assignment is complete, he leaves the glitz and glamour behind and returns to normal reality.

A mistake often made by even the most seasoned bodyguard is the false feeling that the bond he shares with a protectee is long-lasting and has transformed him from employee to friend. When a celebrity hires a protective agent, they are not hiring a friend with muscles or what we term in the industry a "buddyguard." The expectation is that they are hiring an employee, the same as they would hire any other staff member and, therefore, they can and will fire the protector just

---

3. June, Dale L. (2008). *Introduction to Executive Protection* (2nd ed.). Boca Raton: CRC Press, 2008, pp. 141–142.

as quickly. Even after an extended tenure, assuming the celebrity is like family probably will result in getting the rug pulled out from beneath you in the long run. There is only one way to treat the client, and that is professionally, at all times. Be friendly, cordial, and courteous while simultaneously maintaining an emotional wall or distance from the person and their business. While giving due respect to the protectee, personal feelings of emotion toward the person being protected should never become an issue. A large number of careers have been shipwrecked and sunk by falsely assuming that the protectee has a bond extending beyond normal working relationships.

While in the client's world, the bodyguard must refrain from asking for things that might be perceived as overstepping their bounds, such as career assistance or financial loans. Never ask for special favors, and as a rule of thumb, don't discuss negative personal or family circumstances and problems, nor indulge in any overly social activities with the client's family or friends that are outside the bounds of the assignment.

When the assignment comes to a conclusion, the protector says his farewells and goes on his way to further opportunities and clients while maintaining his integrity and reputation. The parting should not be emotional, or with the expectation of some parting gift. In essence, the protector is no longer in the life of the client and he will feel better about the separation of service if he looks at it as simply an assignment which had run its course.

PROTOCOL

When you are in the world of the VIP, there are certain protocols that must be followed, and the easiest to remember and forget is courtesy. Courtesy is more than good manners. It is a way of showing respect, which has the byproduct of producing the same in return. "Please" and "thank you" are the most powerful words in any language. Being gracious and thankful demonstrates appreciation and recognition of regard and thoughtfulness. Unless directed otherwise, it is always appropriate to address the client as "Mr." or "Ms.," "Sir" or "Ma'am," or by an actual official title such as "Senator," "Doctor," and so forth. Do not address the VIP by his or her first name except if directed to do so. For entertainers who use a stage name, make sure that you adhere to that in public or when in the presence of the VIP's guests, friends, and family.

Courtesy extends beyond words. You want to be remembered in the most professional light possible. As such, do not use heavily scented soaps, perfumes, body deodorants, and aftershave lotions. If it is necessary to use an aftershave, use something odorless, such as Aloe vera lotion, which is an excellent skin conditioner with a cooling affect.

When on an expense account for meals, order food as though you were paying for it. Don't order the filet mignon with lobster when a burger with a baked potato will suffice. In other words, do not order the most expensive items simply because someone else is paying for the meal. When meal relief is given or if snacks are available, do not eat in front of the VIP or guests. If the assignment requires eating with the protectee, heed good table manners and do not eat as though the meal is your last meal. It is better to leave the table a little hungry than to stuff yourself and feel the effects later.

BEING THE SHADOW—CLOSE PROXIMITY PROTECTION

There is a belief in the protective services that an agent lives in the shadows of his assignment, going almost everywhere with the client from early morning to late at night. That is the belief; however, in reality, the protector *is* the shadow. He does not only work in the shadow of his client, he in essence becomes the shadow: anticipating, planning, and preparing for all eventualities for the benefit of the safety of those in his charge.

Being the shadow also means knowing the protectee's habits, idiosyncrasies, and even thoughts, to the degree where you can anticipate their next move. Don't overdo it by being too smothering to the client; instead, allow room for them to be in the spotlight, yet figure out the proximity needed to effectively deal with a situation.

ADAPTABILITY, GOOD CHARACTER, AND CRITICAL THINKING

Good character can be defined as consisting of three qualities: good principles (to guide actions), conscience (to internalize those principles), and moral courage (to act on them).

Good character incorporates strengths such as integrity, good work habits, high energy levels, enthusiastic attitude, an ability to relate to all socioeconomic levels, loyalty to the team and those whom one has given his word to. This individual takes responsibility seriously, but does not take himself seriously, and may even be self-effacing at times, yet will have little tolerance for others who will not do their share of the work load.

Critical thinking is the ability to evaluate viewpoints, facts, and behaviors objectively, in order to assess the presentation of information or methods of argumentation, to establish the true worth or merit of an act or a course of conduct. It is systematically evaluating information to reach reasonable conclusions best supported by evidence. In a word, critical thinking means conscious analysis. It is the ability to gain all the facts and then make appropriate conclusions based on those facts. It is seeing the whole or big picture, not just a microcosm.

> Critical thinking includes skills of observation, description, inference, language analysis assessing the role of the frame of reference, and examining unwarranted assumptions or other potential obstacles to clear thinking. To be good thinkers, we need to be observant, watching carefully to get a sense of the big picture, while taking note of the unusual or questionable. We need to be attentive to detail while not losing sight of the larger framework. It is wise not to take anything for granted. There could be serious consequences if we are oblivious, make mistakes, or overlook something.[4]

INTANGIBLE TOOLS

Imagination

It is mentioned elsewhere that the protective agent should have a good imagination, and this can be put to use when beginning an assignment. The agent surveys the scene as it is, then visualizes how it will be when the VIP arrives or is in attendance. Using his imagination, he begins to frame the big picture as it references security requirements. He begins looking at obvious points, then moves to more obscure junctures.

---

4. June, Dale L. (2008). *Introduction to Executive Protection* (2nd ed.). Boca Raton: CRC Press, 2008, pp. 141–142.

In his mind's eye, he asks himself, "If I were planning an attack, how would I do it, when, and where?" Satisfying himself that all potential attack points are covered, he then imagines how, if he were an attacker, he would compromise his own security arrangements, and then he imagines a counter plan as a contingency.

Perspective

No number of people see the same things in the same way. It depends on their point of view or perspective. A bird's-eye view from a height will not provide the same perspective as a street-level view. Physical perspective is distorted by several things: sound or noise, color, lighting, day or night, placement of the sun, movement, a person's education and training, distance, even social status. The recognition of patterns is important as humans follow distinct patterns of behavior. A major focus should be on people and their behaviors: how they interact with others, how they create certain situations, and how they resolve conflicts.

Observation

Observation is seeing, recognizing and reacting. Good observers see things that others fail to see or are naive in recognizing. Often, we see things such as our exit off the freeway, we read the sign, we know it's coming, and still we pass right by, failing to make the exit. This is because we saw but didn't react. It could be the same with an untrained or inexperienced protective agent, seeing a person keeping his hands in his pockets and a scowl on his face, while others are cheering and clapping. He may see it, but not recognize it as the sign of a potential attacker.

Dictionaries will define observation as watching or seeing. For the purpose of our profession, observation should be defined as seeing (or watching), then recognizing what is being seen, and reacting to it. In other words, the head must always be in the game. The eyes can't see what the brain doesn't know; therefore, critical to observation skills is having the right mindset, with that defined as "a fixed mental attitude or disposition that predetermines a person's response to and interpretations of situations."[5] Having a correct mindset is about instant recog-

---

5. American Heritage® Dictionary of the English Language (5th ed.). (2016). Houghton Mifflin Harcourt Publishing Company.

nition of indicators of a circumstance or situation as it develops and being alert to all intents, purposes, and consequences.

To practice improving your observation skills, as you drive your daily route day after day, make a note of the things you see that you have never really noticed before. It may be a color on a building, or a specific type of tree; make note of the vehicles you pass, various makes and models of cars, and so forth. Another exercise is to look at everyone you meet, and in classic Sherlock Holmes fashion, try to make deductions about the person based only from the things you see. When watching a movie, look into the background of the scene, look at the time on a wall clock behind the characters, pay extra attention to the people in the background. In an action or adventure movie, see if you can spot the CGI. While you may be wrong in some of your deductions, your observational skills will undoubtedly improve as a result of the exercises.

As any dedicated observer or perfectionist will tell you, it's all in the details. Trained observers are of a different breed altogether as they see things that the rest of the world generally misses, such as development of patterns, associations, subtle movements, and objects out of place or that don't fit with the environment.

In quickly developing scenarios, there is no time out to think of what is about to happen or has just occurred; instead, the observer must have rapid cognition. Cognitive thinking is reason and recognition combined as a spontaneous and involuntary reaction. Images must pass through the eyes to the brain; if the brain does not recognize what the eyes see, reason cannot occur or it may be delayed. Recognition and reaction are components of reflex action. Reflex means responding to a stimulus (seeing or observing) without thinking.

Attitude

Underlying and affecting the tools of imagination, perspective, and observation is the attitude of the protector. Some see only what they want to see, while others see things others don't see or fail to recognize. If the protector has personal problems causing stress, his mind may be more focused on the problems than on his duties. If he is feeling ill or fatigued, his thoughts may be centered on bed rest and getting well. If he is angry at the protectee or co-workers, his attitude may affect the way he responds to the actions and activities of others. If he feels he is not receiving the respect he believes is his due or he thinks he is underpaid considering his responsibility, he may respond with a decline in his attention to detail and dedication to his assignment.

Conversely, if he is recognized for all his hard work and dedication or believes in himself and how fortunate he is to be part of an elite assignment, he may become inspired to go beyond the call of duty, diving into tasks that no one else desires, but because he understands that someone has to do it, he reasons simply: why not him?

Communication Skills

Verbal and written skills are important and effective tools for a person working in any occupation but are especially important for protective agents, as much of what we do requires collaboration and fostering good relationships. There are liaisons, meetings, confrontations, reports, and instructions that must have eloquent resolutions coming only from clear communication.

A college degree is not normally required to be a protective agent, yet it is an excellent foundation, as the university experience is the breeding ground for creative and critical thinking. While not necessarily a prerequisite, a background in the military or law enforcement is also very helpful in a career of personal protection. Military and law enforcement training provide ingrained discipline, self-motivation, leadership and management skills, and the necessary interpersonal competencies, all of which have their uses in the EP profession.

BEING FLEXIBLE

> If we say we always do something in a certain manner, that means there is never an exception. Circumstances of life dictate that nothing is ever always.
>
> —Dale June

While in the employ of a VIP, the bodyguard, under most circumstances, follows the wants and dictates of the person for whom he is responsible. However, there are many occasions in which he is at liberty to exercise his free will and discretion. An agent with this level of responsibility often makes decisions with no outside influence but is instead guided by his conscience, experience, and training.

Knowing this, we must keep in mind that plans of celebrity clients are constantly changing. Circumstances and situations do not remain static, and your client is within their rights to change their minds about what they want to do, where and when they want to do it, and with whom. Naturally, this will cause the protector to have to abruptly make logistical changes and modify arrangements. A protector must be pragmatic, willing to change and compromise, and learn how to manage and internalize any frustrations. In more simple terms, he must be flexible in adapting to any and all changes. He must be able to think on his feet and become a master at making decisions on the fly.

STAYING ENGAGED

In times of emergency and with ever-changing circumstances, there is no time to reflect or consult a manual, so we must always strive to stay informed and engaged. As fast as the brain's impulses can be fired, the entire scenario can be analyzed with conclusions and recommended solutions.

A maxim of a successful person is, "If you are going to kill time, work it to death." There will be many times in a protective agent's career when he will be standing in hallways or other lonely places with nothing to do but think, all the while being alert to his surroundings. In those times, when ten minutes can feel like two hours, his thoughts will often roam. These are excellent times to stay engaged with mental exercises. If he can imagine a realistic scenario and troubleshoot it, when the time comes that he is presented with a similar scenario, his mind will instantly revert to how his imagination solved the problem previously. He won't have to think, because his mind has already been there and is conditioned to react.

In baseball, a batter waiting in the on-deck circle watches the pitcher and visualizes swinging the bat against a variety of pitches; a basketball player at the free throw line visualizes the path of the ball to the basket before he launches his shot; in football, a placekicker visualizes every kick going through the upright goalpost just before he kicks the ball. Much the same, a protective agent visualizes his reaction in the instance of an attack. In those moments of boredom, the protector can maximize his effectiveness by rehearsing his reaction and response to whatever scenarios he can imagine.

SITUATIONAL AWARENESS

A simple explanation of situational awareness is being aware of those around you and cataloging anything in the environment that could be considered threatening to your safety or the safety of others. The situational awareness color code devised by Jeff Cooper for police officer training has also been adopted into the psyche and practice of the protective agent. There are four levels or colors in the code:

1. *White* is during a period of relaxation, when there is no activity stirring and everything is a time of quietness. There is no reason to be suspicious. In the life of a protective agent, the color white is probably active only when at home, away from the demands of the job.
2. *Yellow* means a higher level of awareness, anticipating that a potential threat may occur, but there are no overt indications of anything suspicious that would lead to a reason to rise to a higher level of awareness. This condition is similar to driving in traffic, aware but having no particular signs of pending trouble. Yellow is a normal cautionary level on a routine day.
3. *Orange* is a level of being aggressively alert because danger has been identified and may erupt. Attention shifts to the point of interest and focus becomes centered.
4. *Red* is the instant when the threat has developed to the point of potential instant execution. All senses are awake, alert for that moment when explosive action calls for full attention and reaction.

SPATIAL AWARENESS

Spatial awareness is having cognitive knowledge or recognition and perspective of distances and things around us in our environment. We wander through life only casually aware of the objects, barriers and people we encounter. Walking down an avenue in New York City during the lunch hour is not an easy task: the sidewalk is jammed with people, yet with awareness of the crowd, the street can be easily navigated. Humans seem to have a built-in radar telling them how to avoid walking into others by dodging, shifting, and sidestepping oncoming pedestrians without missing a beat.

Think of a baseball outfielder and how he knows he is approaching the wall when he crosses from the green field onto the dirt warning track. As he runs closer to the wall, with his eyes up into the sky looking at the ball, he places his hand, the hand without the glove, outstretched toward the wall. As touch is information, he knows how close to hitting the wall he is.

When accompanying a protectee, the bodyguard must be aware of how close he is to many things while at the same time processing a vast amount of sensory input. While scanning for potential danger, he has to devote a portion of his awareness to the distances of objects and individuals around him, such as the stride of the protectee, the distance from the crowds during a scheduled meet and greet, and who's on the other side of a revolving door. In essence, situational and spatial awareness become instinctive measures for alertness and mobility.

Chapter 5

THE WORLD OF MUSIC

In this chapter, the goal is to introduce the protector into the world of music. Not music theory or appreciation, as it's not about our individual tastes in music or musicians; instead, this introduction is from the perspective of the bodyguard. The music industry can be likened to a baked pie, and some pieces are larger than others. The biggest slices consist of touring and recording, followed to various degrees by personal appearances and photo or video shoots. Of course, our role doesn't necessarily end there; depending on the entertainer, we may provide services that extend far beyond when the cameras are rolling.

RECORDING

Almost without question, if you are a musician, the recording process is the part you love. This is where they get to be creative; it's where they take an abstract concept and make it a sonic work of art, one that hopefully will generate revenue. While it can be hard work for the artists, for most it's a labor of love. They have the ability to get paid and earn a living for doing what they enjoy most.

For protectors, particularly with personalities like mine, this part can be as exciting as watching paint dry. And while excitement need not be a prerequisite for the work that a bodyguard does, I think it's fair to say that in the majority of cases, the recording process occurs in a pretty sterile environment, which means our protective posture needs to be modified to fit.

For example, unless some type of information leak occurs or fans spot the arrival, when a protectee goes to the studio, it's traditionally unannounced, creating a degree of anonymity. Recording studios, by their very nature, are pretty well secured on their own. Not necessarily because of the celebrity clientele who come there to record, but because they've got thousands and in some cases millions of dollars' worth of equipment that they want to hold on to. As such, most have some type of in-house security systems in place, ranging from access-controlled doors to uniformed guards and multiplex surveillance cameras.

So essentially, once you facilitate the movement of getting the protectee to the recording studio, your evening might well consist of a whole lot of hurry up and wait. Unless you were hired to play the drums, which is pretty unlikely, you just need to make sure that you are not in the way. With that said, getting out of the way doesn't mean clocking out mentally. As protectors, we have to always remain in the moment, because Murphy's Law will strike the minute you let your guard down.

We have to find a way to continue to keep our edge and maintain our focus for the duration. You might not think that's much of a challenge for a couple of hours, but what about six hours, or ten, or 15? If your VIP is working on a full-length project, this visit isn't just one isolated session. It could actually span several consecutive days, weeks, and even months.

So how do you keep your edge? How do you stay focused? In fact, one of the perks about a recording studio is that many of the nicer ones come packed to the rafters with amenities. Big picture-wise, every studio wants to compete for those recording dollars, particularly with the virtually unlimited budgets that come with major recording stars and their record labels. To do this, the studios have to come up with ways to entice the artists to want to come to their facility versus the one down the street.

One way to accomplish this is to be generous with the amenities. Usually located somewhere in the studio is a very comfortable VIP lounge, stocked with all the food and drink that you can think of, because requiring an artist to have to disrupt the creative process to go out and grab a burger is a waste of time and money. Instead, the studios will have runners who will gladly go out and get whatever you need, no matter the time of day.

In many cases, the food and drink are incorporated into the recording budget as an incidental cost; and, as part of the client's entourage, you often have permission to order what you want as well.

You want burgers? "Fine." You want tacos? "Fine." You want ice cream? "Fine." Imagine, somebody's going to run out and grab that for you and you don't even have to pay for it out of your pocket as it's included in the budget for what the studio charges for the session.

The luxuries extend beyond just food and drink. Almost all studios have cable or satellite TV with thousands of stations. Many have pool and ping pong tables and virtually every video game console system on the market. Now, these things in theory are for the client, but the reality is that, outside of the food and drink, the client doesn't take part in much, because they're usually so wrapped up in the process of doing what they love, namely creating their new music. As a result, the people who usually get to take advantage of all these amenities are the celebrities' entourage, and while that might be large or small depending on the protectee, one constant in that equation is usually you.

So, let's recap: it's a secure location, you know you need to be out of the way, and it's okay to partake in the amenities. With this in mind, you've located the VIP lounge and found its comfortable couch, the AC is on full blast, and you've ordered one of everything on the menu. You're good and focused for the first three hours—for five hours—for eight hours. But that was only day 1. How about hour 12 on day 16? Nothing out of the ordinary has happened in all this time, so it's okay to loosen up and relax a little bit, right?

Think about it: you've had nothing going on for hours on end, with the recording process running into the wee hours night after night. Your feet have been hurting all day, so you decide to slip your shoes off for a bit. With the air conditioner blowing, and your stomach full of pasta, your head starts to tilt back. Those eyelids start to get heavy, and that voice in the back of your head goes, "it's for just a little bit—nothing has happened here for over two weeks."

Now, Murphy's Law could manifest itself in something catastrophic happening, but that's more of a remote possibility. What's much more likely to happen is that just when you decide to take that quick ten-minute power nap, that's when the client's manager walks in with a record executive from the label. From his perspective, viewing you with head tilted back and snoring, he doesn't look at this as just an isolated ten minutes over a two-week period. Instead, what he sees is a person he's hired and is paying, who not only doesn't have anything strenuous to do all day long, but to add insult to injury, is sleeping on the job with his shoes off, surrounded by empty candy wrappers with Cinemax Late Night blaring on the TV. Welcome to your last day on the job.

In this setting, your mission is to figure out, in whatever way works for you, how you're going to stay engaged and keep your focus. I'll admit, based off of my personality type, the recording process is pretty grueling for me, but my method is to keep myself busy with paperwork. I work on everything from scheduling, to company payroll, to planning the Advance for the next assignment. Unlike many, I'm also a person who can read and not fall asleep, which is a big plus. You have to find what works for you and use that to help you figure out how to stay in the moment. I'm not saying that you can't eat or watch TV; only the strictest of clients would have an issue with that in this setting. Just remember that you are still being paid to do a job, and appearances count.

TOURING

In many ways, touring is the flip side of recording in terms of pacing, responsibilities, and workload. These days, touring makes up arguably the largest slice of the pie as it relates to interactions in the music business. If you are interested in doing celebrity protection, particularly in working for musicians, this is where you are going to earn your bread and butter.

The reality is, music doesn't sell like it used to, primarily because of the dramatic increase in digital piracy. Unscrupulous individuals bootleg the music, and the sales don't make it back to the record company or the artist. Additionally, there are now a multitude of digital music streaming services such as Apple Music, Spotify, and Tidal, where you just pay one low monthly fee and you can listen to every album that has ever been created since the invention of the record player. Less music being sold means that artists aren't making money like they used to from their percentages of album sales.

The stopgap for this is to supplement that decreasing revenue by putting an increased focus on touring. If an artist might have gone out previously and done a 15-day promotional tour to support the pending release of a new album, today they go out for 30 days. Subsequently, one tour now leads right into the next tour, to the next tour, and the next. What this also means is that there is always a need for protectors on the touring side of the music business.

Music touring is also a great way to break into the industry as a whole. Because there are so many moving parts to a tour, there is a need beyond someone just standing right next to the protectee, which is what most traditionally think of when it comes to bodyguards. One way that aspiring individuals can get their foot in the door is by working venue tour security. Now, when I say venue security, I don't mean event security, aka the guys in the yellow shirts positioned in the front of the stage or standing in the aisles checking tickets. While there is nothing wrong with that, what I'm specifically talking about is what is termed in the touring markets as "Back of House" (BOH) security.

When a major tour comes into a city, the venue itself sometimes has a need for someone in a security role to handle what's happening backstage. Oftentimes, that person works for the show, concert or tour promoter, not the artist, and they are tasked with making sure that the promoter's investment—the things that happen backstage—all run smoothly and that a trained eye is on the lookout for potential liability issues.

Venue tour security interfaces with the artist's bodyguard, in many cases before the protector even sets foot in that city. They can be the protector's eyes and ears, and I know a number of people who not only excel in that role but are making a great career out of it.

For example, if I'm on tour with a client, and I observe an agent who is exceptionally good at his duties while at the venue, there have been occasions in the past when I have picked that individual up for future assignments. Therefore, back of house security is a great way to get noticed, as there are many decision-makers that you will encounter, from bodyguards and agency owners to tour managers and show promoters. Imagine the lead person with Acme Promotions noticing you and appreciating your work demeanor and professionalism. He knows that in less than one month he has another tour coming with an even bigger artist, and what better way to protect his investment than to work with someone he has used before?

Essentially, back of house security is a way to work for a particular promoter or venue, creating a revenue stream and gaining experience working around celebrities and other protectors. The ambitious will also see it as a way to break into working for the tour itself by becoming a member of the artist's close protection detail. For example, on a recent international tour that I ran, I had three agents who handled just the venues. They were ultimately responsible for all of the things that happen backstage prior to the protectee coming into that space. Because the tour itself had multiple artists, and each of these multiple artists had their own security staff, the BOH security employed by my firm were responsible for interfacing with multiple security teams, making sure that each of them were up to speed and knew what was happening at that location.

This meant that they handled a list of things that ranged from credentialing to making sure that the house security and special event staff were briefed on how we do things. They made sure that the local law enforcement was up to speed on what we were doing and were comfortable with the plan. They observed the venue screening procedures (bag searches, magnetometers, etc.) and made sure they were handled correctly and in accordance with our contractual agreement.

BOH venue security, as you can see, is a highly specialized area in and of itself, but it's also a great way to get in to the business, No, you may not necessarily be standing right next to the protectee, so if that's your barometer of success, you may feel slighted. However, there are many different avenues to success in the protection industry, and this business can take you some amazing places.

PERSONAL APPEARANCES

For all but the most reclusive artist, personal appearances are deeply ingrained into the duties that musicians know they are required to perform. Let's face it, outside of doing their work just for the sake of art, they create a product, and that product has to be marketed and promoted. Making personal appearances is a big part of how music gets sold to the buying public.

When the entertainer goes on the *Today* show, or *Good Morning America,* or *Jimmy Kimmel* or *The Ellen DeGeneres* show, somebody's got to make all the logistics happen. While Artist Management is probably making the schedule, someone has to help enforce it, and formally or informally, that role often falls on us, the protectors. While you might ask what this has to do with security, the simple answer is that it all comes down to logistics.

Imagine the celebrity client has an album coming out at the end of the week, so she is booked by the record label to do the talk show circuit to promote it. Keep in mind, however, that *Late Night with Steven Colbert* is in New York, but the *Tonight Show with Jimmy Fallon* is in Los Angeles. The need for two back-to-back appearances on opposite coasts is a logistical challenge, and someone has to be responsible for the timetable. You have to get to the show, you have to do the musical performance, and perhaps there is an autograph signing with a meet-and-greet with the fans afterwards. Speaking solely about transportation, you have to get the client in the vehicle, you have to navigate heavy traffic in Manhattan to get to the always-crowded JFK Airport. Once there, you have to navigate through the airport, and you have to coordinate arrivals with the vehicle and driver on the other end. Upon landing, you have to navigate the paparazzi at LAX, then once in the car, fight through Los Angeles traffic. Once you get there and get the VIP on set, you still have to do all the activities mentioned earlier. Oh, and upon conclusion, you find that Management has just booked the *Today Show* back in NYC, so you need to do this all over again in reverse.

As a protector in the celebrity arena, you likely play a vital part with each of those movements, because if your client is late, who is going to get the phone call? You are. When you get off the plane and the driver isn't there, who are they going to look at for answers (or to assess blame)? Logistics, troubleshooting, problem solving and crisis management—effective protection agents will find themselves doing this much more than jumping in front of bullets. Knowing this, it stands to reason that those who do it well will be the ones the client is going to call time and again.

PHOTO SHOOTS

Another way musicians promote their product is photo shoots. There are two types of photo shoots: studio and location. Studio shoots are the ones that occur on a set, in a controlled environment like a photography studio. For these, our job is just basically facilitating a movement: get the client to the studio and then just fall back into the shadows.

Location shoots, on the other hand, can be extremely busy and challenging. We will cover them in greater detail in the corresponding chapter on the movie industry. This is because filming an actor for a film or television project is a lot like photographing a musician for a photo shoot, at least in terms of what we do in our role as protectors.

PERSONAL TIME

Musicians are people, too, and they do things on their personal time just like everyone else. As such, expect them to go shopping, eat dinner out, go to the park with their children, or walk the dog. Your work as a bodyguard includes giving them the chance to have somewhat of a normal life by ensuring their safety and security wherever they go. The concept of downtime can mean different things for the client than it does for the protector. Even when they're not in star mode, you still have to take your responsibilities seriously, because the need for our services includes wherever they are, not just on stage.

WORKING WITH THE ENTOURAGE

One of the most unique challenges in working in the world of music is dealing with the entourage. By and large, the majority of successful (and not so successful) musicians travel with a retinue of people. There is an entire apparatus that moves with them, each with their respective roles, some very necessary, some not so much. As the one person always with the client, you will have constant interactions with the entourage. Whether those interactions will be positive or negative is up for grabs, but rest assured, these individuals can directly or indirectly make your assignment a shining success or a living hell.

While time will be spent discussing the official roles of select individuals of the client's inner circle, for now we focus on the members of the entourage who do not have a specific duty. These are the friends, cousins, girlfriends, and hangers-on who find themselves moving with the bubble. While the client is usually focused on engaging in their craft, the entourage gets to enjoy all the fringe benefits, and unfortunately in many cases, also end up getting in the way. Situations like this can quickly lead to annoyance on our part, and in a short time it's easy to end up having an antagonistic relationship with them. However, executive protection is a business, and politics play a part in this business. I'm not talking about protecting politicians who are dignitaries, but interpersonal politics – understanding relationships and human nature when working with the entourage. Remember, the entourage may have the client's ear in a way that you do not. In many cases, they have known the client longer, they can talk to him or her frankly, and they can be very opinionated on a variety of things—including, for instance, recommending somebody who they are sure can do your job cheaper and better than you.

With that in mind, we have to be careful about alienating the entourage, even though they might get under our skin. Protectors at times will have to play politics with someone we don't particularly like, or whose function in the client's circle remains a mystery. Using the tools at our disposal, we need to mold the entourage from troublesome annoyance into a working component contributing to the overall success of the mission.

The solution to this problem is found in the art of verbal judo.[1,2]

Verbal Judo has a main theme of generating voluntary compliance, through verbal persuasion and maintaining "professional face." This is maintaining a professional demeanor, even in the presence of insults. The three goals are:

1. Safety—to use words to prevent confrontations from going off the rails where the opponent shuts down or becomes physically violent;
2. Professionalism—Recognize the impact of words and use language appropriate to each encounter. Your opponent then begins to view things from your vantage point.
3. Reduced liability—Handling encounters more skillfully, one is less likely to generate complaints and will also allow for his opponent to be more articulate in describing his reasoning and actions.[3]

---

1. Retrieved 12/26/17 from en.wikipedia.org/wiki/Verbal self defense

Verbal judo is defined as using one's words to prevent, de-escalate, or end an attempted assault. It is a way of using words as a way to maintain mental and emotional safety.

2. Uvhe, Ugo. How To Use Verbal Judo; Defusing Hostile Situations Through Conversations. *Psychology Today* (8/15/2012), Retrieved 06.22/18.

This is the essence of how verbal judo works, redirecting hostile energy directed towards you, and influencing an aggressor to think on your terms. This is done with genuine compassion towards the aggressor and genuine confidence in yourself. It is a process of getting people to transition from thinking with their reptilian brain to thinking with their pre frontal cortex.

3. Scott, Brian. (2000, August 1). Verbal Judo: Talk Your Way Through Confrontations. *Police Magazine*. Retrieved 12/26/17 from policemag.com/channel/patrol/articles/2000/08/verbal-judo-talk-your-way-through-confrontations.aspx

While challenging, if you can get the entourage on your side, it will not only work in your favor by giving you one less thing to worry about; they can actually become a force-multiplier for you. While it's certainly annoying when they ask you for an extra wristband so their girl-of-the-moment can come into the VIP section, the following day, when the client opens his hotel room door, sees you out there and says he wants that triple mocha pistachio deluxe with caramel on top, you can say to a member of the entourage, "Will you do me a favor? The boss wants this." And while they're getting the overpriced treat, you are free to remain on-post to perform your primary role of protecting the client.

As a solo operator, meaning it's just you as the lone protector instead of the more ideal situation of functioning within a team of two or more, we always want to have laid eyes on a place before we bring the protectee into that particular area. However, that's tough to do when you also need to be arm's length away guarding the client. Using the entourage to your advantage is an ingenious way to effectively be two places at once.

For example, in a pinch, you can send them over to the venue early with a specific set of questions to be answered. What's the interior layout? What's the phone number of the manager of this restaurant that we're going to? Are there paparazzi camped out in front of the hotel? and so forth. It's not the most ideal situation, but it's better than going into an environment effectively blind. Admittedly, you can only hope to get this kind of cooperation if you have earned the respect of the entourage and that has to come from by diplomacy and understanding human behavior.

COPING WITH LONG HOURS

There is no sugarcoating this: in the world of celebrity and VIP protection, the days can run quite long. The best way to illustrate this is by giving you a real-world example. Several years back, I had a wonderful gentleman come to work for me. He came from a law enforcement background and was transitioning over into EP. Most of his assignments were short-term domestic jobs. I know he was really chomping at the bit to spread his wings and do more. During that period, our firm had a client who was a recognized television personality. The nature of the show took the VIP to exotic places around the world to film. During this season, we had to provide security for eight weeks of filming, and due to budget restrictions, I could only send one agent from the company, having to rely on local staff for additional resources.

Due to the grueling pace of the shoot schedule, I elected to split the assignment into two four-week sessions. I sent a seasoned agent out for the first half, and the gentleman in question, who you'll recall really wanted more field work, went out there for the second half. As our protocol mandates, he would send me periodic updates. The first day, he said, "We did this; we did that; I'm pumped up; I'm all about it."

The third day, he said, "We did this, and we did that; there are some long days and nights, but I'm focused." About a week into it, I noticed a downshift in the enthusiasm of the updates.

Why did he lose his enthusiasm? Well, here's how the days went for that assignment: They first flew to Europe, and then would fly or drive to the various cities on the shooting schedule. Once there, protocol was to get the client to the hotel, then advance the various locations the VIP would be going to; for example, the beach or a restaurant. At the designated time, we would take the protectee to these locations for filming, then afterwards return the client back to the hotel, where they generally napped. During that time, the team would advance the sites where the next scenes were to be shot. By the very nature of the show, the segments almost always ended in a nightclub, so that necessitated shooting late nights. More often than not, once the client was brought to the party, and the shooting wrapped, the VIP remained at the club, enjoying the atmosphere and all that came with it.

So, a day might begin around 7 a.m. and they might wrap at 2, 3, or 4 a.m.—and then have to go to the next city early the next day and start it all over again. Picture eight weeks of this, keeping in mind that this particular VIP could have written the book about how to party like a rock star.

Consider the fact that when you're out doing advances, the client gets to rest. When you're traveling from point A to point B, the client is in the car sleeping or on the boat sleeping or on the plane sleeping, but you need to be up. So, imagine an operational pace of little to no sleep; plus, there's all the stress that comes from being in a foreign country and even the inconvenience of communicating with your agency and family in a different time zone.

The assignment ended safely and the agent returned back stateside exhausted but accomplished. Fast forward to approximately a year after that; he came into my office to speak to me about this opportunity that came to him from a financial institution to do protection for the CEO. He explained that the hours were a traditional Monday through Friday with weekends off, with his primary routine consisting of picking his protectee up in the morning at 7 a.m. and bringing him to the bank. Once on the premises, he had an office where he waited until needed. At the end of the day, he escorted the protectee home, leaving at 5:00 p.m., giving him the freedom to eat dinner with his family nightly and at a reasonable hour. The only time this particular executive did any traveling was once a year when he ventured out of his home state to attend the company's annual board meeting. The agent also saw this as an opportunity to spend some quality time with his children. While I was sad to see him go, I wholeheartedly endorsed the transition, as it created an avenue of growth for the agent.

A month or so later, we grabbed lunch together, and I asked how things were going. He mentioned that it was by all accounts great: his assignment consisted of picking up the client, taking him to work, waiting nearby, and then escorting him home. After getting all of that out, there was a bit of a pause followed by, "but sometimes I have to admit I can get bored out of my mind."

While humorous, the pros outweighed the cons: he noted that he got to eat dinner with his family every night and had a social life again on the weekends. The move actually had a hidden blessing, as there was a serious illness in the family, and he was around to be able to help with that. Imagine the torment a husband and father would feel if he were on the other side of the world during a family crisis.

This story has always seemed the perfect anecdote to contrast the pace of working on the celebrity side versus corporate. Both have their pluses and minuses, yet it is up to the individual protector to do an honest self-assessment to determine what would be the best fit for him or her.

DEALING WITH TEMPTATIONS

While it might sound cliché, the music business is rife with sex, drugs, and rock and roll. You can run from it screaming, or you can acknowledge it as an occupational hazard and adjust accordingly.

Let's start with the obvious one, the groupies. I'll say this to you now: the minute you start working with a high-profile celebrity, you will suddenly become the sexiest guy or girl in the world. In fact, you will get hit on and complimented so much that you may even start believing it and thinking that you ought to pursue a career in modeling.

News flash: that attention is not really about you. They are hitting on you to get close to the VIP, and that's a situation that many in our industry end up failing to once they lose sight of that. Agents who've had extremely good opportunities with long-term assignments let that one area of temptation mess them up. In the intelligence business, it's called the honey trap. So, while it may seem self-explanatory, this is a business that will put you in the same room with Victoria's Secret models, Playboy Bunnies, and a nightclub full of attractive women who would do anything to get invited into the VIP section. Don't fall for it.

Another example about temptation is one you might not readily think of: free stuff, or as they call it in the entertainment industry, swag. One thing I've always found interesting is that for some reason, people always want to give wealthy people things for free. It's an interesting phenomenon: high net-worth individuals like celebrities have plenty of money, but they get all kinds of stuff for free, sometimes by the truckload. A by-product of that is that you as a protector sometimes get gifts for free just by association. Speaking from experience, I can say that I haven't bought a pair of sneakers since about 2002. Additionally, I have jeans in my closet that have never been worn, with the tags still on them. So, if I just admitted that I have benefited from swag, why do I put it in this chapter on temptation like it's a negative?

Here's the problem, again best illustrated by an example: imagine an entrepreneur who has an emerging wristwatch company. He's trying to break into the market, the celebrity market, and he approaches you and says, "Hey, I've got this brand-new watch coming out in the fall, and it's going to take the world by storm. I'm trying to see if your client will be interested in checking out the brand. If he is, I'll give him the version with the diamonds in it for free. And just for you showing it to him and helping break the ice, I'll give you a less expensive version of the watch (minus the diamonds)."

Let's take the scenario a step further. You show the client the watch, just *show* him, and he likes it. Next week is the American Music Awards, and your client walks the red carpet. While there, the various members of the media ask what he's wearing and notice his fabulous new timepiece. They ask him what kind of watch he's wearing, and he lets them know about this new company called ABC Watches.

The next day, you get a phone call from the musician's manager. And the manager asks you if you were the contact between the client and the watch rep. You mumble something about how you simply passed the information on, and the manager says, "Thank you very much, but your services are no longer required." And just like that, you find yourself fired.

The reason for that abrupt termination? Well, unbeknownst to you, your harmless introduction just scuttled their multimillion endorsement deal with Rolex that was on the table. Now, you didn't know that the client had an endorsement deal in the works. However, your actions led to a highly visible public appearance with the competing watch brand, and that led to the other company feeling slighted and backing out.

My rule of thumb is, if someone offers me something for the client or for myself, they need to take it to management first. I thank them for their kind offer but explain that they need to discuss it directly with management first as a matter of protocol. If the manager chooses to extend some swag this way, then that's a legitimate perk, not something I received by making a side deal.

Here's the reason swag isn't a bad word and can actually be a good thing. Let's say your celebrity client has an endorsement deal with Nike; Nike doesn't want the VIP's protector walking around next to the client all day where they are sure to be photographed wearing a competitor of theirs like Adidas. Yet as a protector, I'm not going to be expected to purchase a new wardrobe every time the client secures a different endorsement deal. So, if Nike wants to send some athletic apparel and footwear to me, few would have an issue. However, the first step is directing that inquiry to management for approval and to cover your own bases.

WORKING AWAY FROM HOME

In addition to working long hours, more often than not the business requires us to be away from home for days, weeks, and even months. The extended periods are tough on a protector whose relationship status would be classified as single. It's magnified ten-fold for those agents who have families.

Traveling the world on assignment can be truly exciting. You get to meet people and experience places that you may never have thought you'd ever see. But even the most beautiful of things lose their luster over time, and the only thing you want to see after a long stretch on the road is your own bed.

This is especially a problem for solo practitioners, because you can't delegate aspects of the mission to someone else. If you're fortunate enough to establish a long-term relationship with a client, a relationship where they trust you to protect them, there is a good chance that you are going to be on the road when they are. Keep in mind that the increase in touring in the music industry also means lots of miles logged and stamps in the passport.

CHALLENGING CLIENTS

Many times, the protectee and the client are not one and the same. You may even be hired to provide services to someone who doesn't necessarily want you there. Not all VIPs take kindly to a shadow following them all hours of the day and night, being privy to their actions and confidential/personal conversations outside of the public eye. In these instances, they are merely being tolerant because their celebrity makes having you there a necessary nuisance. They don't understand your mission or procedures and have no interest in learning, and this can make the work environment much more difficult than it has to be.

In one (of many) horror stories, a high-profile VIP had a very low opinion of her protective squad. At times she would do whatever she could do to dodge and lose the detail, making it their responsibility to keep up with her with little or no notice. One morning, she attempted to sneak out of the hotel to take a brisk morning walk with friends. The two agents assigned to her saw her leaving the hotel and followed at a discrete distance.

Along the popular street they were walking, she noticed the agents and appeared to be actively trying to lose them. Later that day, she dismissed the agents, saying their services were no longer needed, as she could get around just fine on her own.

Here's a dirty little secret of the protection business; when working with celebrity clients, success or failure may not always be based on your performance. There are times where it's more about that particular client's temperament. You can do everything right from the beginning, but if the client has a bad day, and you make even the slightest of missteps on that day, it's entirely possible that you won't have a job at the end of it.

What if, behind the scenes, they just lost out on a multimillion-dollar endorsement deal, and that's the same day you missed a turn and got stuck in traffic on the way to the airport and now have to rush or miss the flight? The next ticket issued might be your flight home. It's unfair, but it is a reality. Of course, the best way to counter that is to not give them a reason to take their frustrations out on you. Keep on top of your game, stick to the shadows when not needed, and try to keep things running smoothly for your clients even (and especially) when they have bad days. Be the rock they can lean on, the one person who remains reliable even when others let them down.

In the corporate world, there are business norms and practices; for example, an HR department and tiers of supervisors to work out issues and grievances. These same structures advise the principal when they are making a brash decision and make them aware of the ramifications of such. Those kinds of built-in controls in the corporate environment are rare in celebrity circles; without that defined infrastructure, decisions can at times be rash and not well thought out.

Let's say you're working with a celebrity client. You take him to the record company where he has a big meeting with an executive to discuss renegotiating his fee for the next album. You wait outside, and when the meeting is over an hour later, the client comes out, you escort him to the vehicle, and when you walk up to the car door and pull the handle, the door doesn't open, because the driver forgot to disengage the lock. The VIP is standing there for only the briefest of moments, but it's long enough for the paparazzi to take a couple of pictures before the doors unlock and you put the protectee in the car and depart. The next day, you get a phone call from the client's representatives saying your services are no longer needed.

Was that really because the door was briefly locked? Unlikely. What you weren't privy to was that in the meeting, the record company mentioned that they would not be increasing the recording advance because they just did not believe in the artist and his material as they had in the past. And just like that, a sizable payday for your client was reduced considerably.

So, when he walks out of that room, and that door doesn't open up quickly enough, everything that happened in that meeting just fell on you. While it is not fair, unfortunately, it does happen. As the old saying goes, it's show business.

MORALS AND ETHICAL DILEMMAS

Ethics are defined as the moral expression of integrity, trustworthiness, empathy, and understanding. In essence, ethics are about how people's actions, traditions, and beliefs interact with various situations and may play a part in conflicts or crisis resolution. In this way, consideration is given to the roles of feelings, conscience, obligations, consequences, ideas, and moral responsibility. Ethics are founded on the general principles of the seven cardinal virtues. The four cardinal virtues, from ancient Greek philosophy, are prudence (good judgment), justice, temperance (meaning restriction or restraint), and courage (or fortitude). The three theological virtues are faith, hope, and charity (or love).

It should go without saying that a professional protector should strive to be an ethical person, and therefore should possess the cardinal virtues. Unfortunately, by merely being human, he or she also possesses the potentiality of the seven deadly sins.

When discussing ethics, the seven cardinal virtues cannot be mentioned without recognizing their opposites. Those are:

1. Envy—the desire to have an item or experience that someone else possesses.
2. Gluttony—excessive ongoing consumption of food or drink.
3. Greed or Avarice—an excessive pursuit of material possessions.
4. Lust—an uncontrollable passion or longing, especially for sexual desires.
5. Pride—excessive view of one's self without regard to others.

6. Sloth—excessive laziness or the failure to act and utilize one's talents.
7. Wrath—uncontrollable feelings of anger and hate towards another person.

ETHICAL DILEMMAS

Nothing can be true and false (or right and wrong) at the same time, in the same place in the same way. Thus, a dilemma may be born.

An ethical dilemma is a difficult situation in which an individual is unable to make a decision, due to moral conflicts. Picking one solution would mean undermining another.

To resolve an ethical dilemma, one must consider what the right thing is to do, or what will do the most good with the least harm. An essential element to answering those questions is making the decision after carefully considering all the possible consequences. Every action we take or fail to take has consequences, and as such, eight sets of consequences have been identified:

1. Beneficial/Harmful
2. Long Term/Short Term
3. Obvious/Subtle
4. Instant/Delayed
5. Physical/Emotional
6. Intentional/Unintentional
7. Moral/Ethical/Legal
8. Requiring further Action/Inaction.

News flash—if you have a strict anti-drug stance, celebrities who are notorious for using drugs probably shouldn't be the clients you aspire to work for. It stands to reason that, just during the course of going about your business protecting them, you're going to come into contact with some type of illegal substances, and eventually will have to deal with the actions and behaviors of the people affected by the drugs used.

What if you have a strong religious background, and your protectee is an avowed atheist who says and does things that violate principles of faith that you hold dear? The textbook answer is for you to remind yourself, "I'm just here to do a job." However, the reality of it is that, when you feel strongly about something on a moral level, it can affect your performance. Personal ethics are up to the individual. What you will have to decide is whether you can deal with the ethical issues that a particular client presents. It's inevitable in some shape or form: you are going to be faced with situations where your ethics are challenged, and it's going to be up to you to decide how you are going to deal with that. So, whether that's drugs, racial or political opinions, or any other controversy, something's going to happen where your personal ethics are going to be challenged, and you will have to decide how you are going to react.

In an ironic case of shooting the messenger, there was an extremely wealthy client who held a very strong stance against drugs. He was adamant in his words and actions that drugs had no place in his home or around him and his entourage. One day his director of security discovered at least two persons in the client's personal inner circle were using drugs; the information was given to the client, who said he would take care of it. Surprisingly, the next day the security agent was dismissed, apparently for whistleblowing.

While we can't all pick and choose our clients, set yourself up for success: don't wait until you're already out on assignment with a protectee who has an issue that you knew about (or suspected) in advance. Developing a client profile will help with that. Some celebrities are always getting in trouble, and usually you will know what kind of trouble they get in before you sign on with them. If you go in willingly, then when that behavior does happen, it shouldn't be a surprise for you. Just as we advance an area before we bring our protectee into it, you want to do an advance on potential clients. Don't put yourself, your career, or even your life in jeopardy because of willful actions on the VIP's part that you have strong concerns about from the onset. Have you heard the phrase, "all money isn't good money?" It's true here as well.

GIVING AND RECEIVING GIFTS

A perplexing question a protective agent may face is the appropriateness of giving or receiving gifts to/from the person he is protecting. A good rule of thumb is to decline, as it keeps a can of worms closed that might best be avoided. There could be obvious exceptions such as birthdays and Christmas, and in instances of illness or injury. In the end, it will ultimately depend on the relationship between the VIP and the protector.

One standard that can be implemented is that, when the client offers a gift to the protector, it may be accepted individually if the whole detail also receives gifts; that way, the appearance of favoritism doesn't create discord. However, in any case, if the gift is given to an individual agent, it should be reported to the senior agent on the detail or agency manager. It is not unusual in some instances for a protectee to provide a bonus or gifts of appreciation to the people who have been protecting him or when the assignment comes to a successful end; however, this should always be routed and handled through senior management if you are working through someone else.

On one occasion, a client gave his entire entourage, including his security team, a gift as appreciation for all their hard work and dedication in a very unique manner: the VIP took the security team to a shooting range, where he then replaced a paper target downrange with the wristwatch of one of the agents on the detail. The challenge was to see who was proficient enough to hit the face of the watch at a set distance. After a few rounds of misses at 25 yards, the watch was finally hit, blasting into pieces and leaving the protector watch-less. With a laugh, the client then opened his briefcase, which was filled with significantly more expensive Rolex watches that he then proceeded to give to every member of the protective detail.

MUSIC RESOURCES

Now let's talk about some of the marketing resources available to those interested in the music industry. In all of these, don't expect that clients will find you, at least in the beginning. Instead, you will need to do the leg work in identifying and pitching them. The good news is that it's not as hard as you might think, if you are persistent in your efforts.

Management Agencies

The first resource for you to consider if you want to break into or find more work in the music business is the management agency or personal manager. This entity is usually responsible for the day-to-day direction in an artist's career. It's the personal manager who guides and advises the artists, sets up the deals, figures out what shows they're going to do, determines which appearances they're going to make, and ultimately how to take their client's career to the next level.

Knowing the above, it stands to reason that these people will also play a role in recommending security. They're running almost every aspect of the artist's professional life (and sometimes personal life). Aside from personal managers, the management agency also headquarters the business managers who handle finances. Since these individuals spend a great deal of time reading contracts and signing checks, you certainly want them to know who you are.

So how would you go about finding an artist's management so you can let them know who you are? While Google is certainly your friend in allowing you to do a search online, beware of results that range from out-of-date to just plain irrelevant.

My position is, if you want to know who an artist's management is, there's a simple solution: buy the music, either the physical CD or digital download, along with the booklet. This will not only give you some additional insight into the client, but most importantly, the credits are right there inside the booklet. Managers, be they a one-stop-shop or larger firms, get their contributions acknowledged just like anyone else on the project, so they will be listed in the credits. Also, chances are if they represent one artist, they are also looking to get the next big thing to sign with them, which potentially means future clientele for you.

Once you have the person's name, then you have to figure out your approach. Some managers are brand-new to the business; they might have been this artist's buddy a week ago, and now they represent their creative and financial interests. Those new ones are relatively easy to get to if you can identify them; however, managers who have been in the business for a very long time or have very high-powered rosters may be quite a bit tougher. One method would be to try and schedule an appointment with their assistant or other gatekeeper so you can talk about your services.

You need to develop your own approach, but one thing I can recommend is to find out who the assistant or the assistant's assistant is, and start working your way up from there. It's usually those staff members who want to have the solutions for when a problem comes up;

i.e., "This bodyguard isn't working out, do you know anyone?" If that question ever comes up in an agency, you want your name to be included in the conversation.

The Record Company

The next one up is the record company itself. Artists with a budget that can justify a security expense are usually signed to a record label, which can range from a huge conglomerate to an indie start-up. Again, finding them is easy: they will be listed prominently in the album credits.

So now that you know which record company an artist is working with, who do you talk to there? While your initial thought might be the HR department, they're not likely to hire bodyguards for their artists. What they would be looking for, if anything, is security for the building itself or perhaps, in some instances with larger corporations, for their executives.

The truth of the matter is that reaching individuals with hiring authority for the role you are going after is going to be a challenge. From aspiring artists who want their demo heard, to producers who swear they are the next great hit-maker, most record companies are inundated with calls and mail all the time. As such, the companies already have a system in place to filter that out, and it usually begins with phone prompts and ends with, "please contact us on our website."

My suggestion is, if you are trying to get the attention of the labels, seek out someone in the A&R department. In the music business, that stands for Artist and Repertoire. While an archaic term, this department is vital to the label, because these individuals are responsible for developing the artist's career. They're responsible for matching that singer up with the songwriter and for matching that songwriter up with the music producer, and so forth. They are the department that shepherds an artist through the label system until they get the final product, which is the album, going out the door and into the consumers' hands. It stands to reason that they might also have input or some influence in hiring or recommending security.

In an effort to prevent sounding a bit repetitive, at this stage the reader will know where to find out who the A&R person for a specific artist is. It makes sense that the person responsible for discovering an artist or putting together a (potentially) hit album also wants their name listed in the credits. Buy the music, and you'll likely see their name on it.

It's going to take a little bit of leg work to establish contact, but the reality is, it doesn't cost you anything beyond the price of the product, and if that's too much, try an afternoon of browsing the shelves in the music section of the electronics store.

Publicists

The next marketing target for you to consider is the publicists. If you are wondering why publicists have influence over selecting security, think of it like this: when something bad happens to a public figure, who is the person who makes the statement to the press? Chances are when something goes wrong and damage control is needed, the publicist is brought into the loop early. So, if the issue is even remotely security-related, their input holds weight.

So, when a client has to hire security because something has gone wrong and it hits the newswire—maybe there's a stalker, or they had a bad breakup with a spouse—it's the publicist on the front line for that. If the previous security was involved in a PR disaster (and by now we've read some of the horror stories), the VIP is going to be scrambling for recommendations for new security. In scenarios such as this, it pays to have a relationship with publicists, because anytime there is a crisis, they are front and center in dealing with it. Publicists for up-and-coming artists are also a good target market, because someone will need to hire the security the first time that the artist merits having a higher level of protection.

Of this list of potential contacts, publicists are the easiest to identify and locate because of the very nature of their work. They are going to make it extremely easy to find them, for two reasons: one, if there is a problem, they want reporters working on the story to be able to quickly locate them so they can give a statement. And two, just like everyone else, publicists also want new clients, so if word gets out that they represent Superstar A, that makes them more attractive to Superstar B.

Like the reporters, you might also want to reach out to a publicist when something has gone wrong. Say you read an article about somebody royally screwing up or about a new artist who's rapidly gaining steam; the publicist's name will be right there in the article quoted as the artist's spokesperson. An ambitious protector might reach out to that publicist and see if you can help them solve part of the problem. While this approach might feel a little bit like ambulance chasing, if you are providing a quality service, few would find fault.

With that said, it's best to try to establish relationships with the publicists before bad things happen; this way, they'll think about you when the problem occurs, not just when it hits the paper three days later.

Like the artist management and the staff at the record companies, good publicists are busy people, and with the larger ones, everybody is always trying to get their attention. Use the earlier-mentioned approach of discovering who the assistant or interns are. Find out who's next up to bat and become that person's trusted security contact.

Industry Peers

One of the best ways to break into security work in the music industry is to network with your industry peers. These are people who are already doing the work that you want to do, so pick their brains about it.

As a rule of thumb, I always say that anybody who needs a bodyguard already has a bodyguard. So, unless someone abruptly got terminated and you just happened to be on the scene, you're not going to magically get an account by being in the same room with a VIP. Instead, a better approach might be to try offer your assistance to the current account holder, with the challenge being getting that someone to give you a chance.

Trust is hard to come by with many veterans in the business, as there are just too many unknowns. People inflate their skill sets and level of experience, and the time to find that out is not while you are on assignment. Another unfortunate reality is that poaching is also a problem. No one wants to spend years developing a client only to see the next hotshot breeze in and undercut the rates to be more attractive to a business manager scrambling to cut back on client spending.

To counter this, you have to show industry peers that you are a potential asset, not a liability. One way to do this is to show them that you've attended and completed training from industry-recognized courses. That means that you've made a commitment to the craft in the way of time and money and are serious about the business.

Additionally, peers in the industry want to see some kind of track record before they take a chance on you; however, it's admittedly difficult to build a track record if you are just starting out. One option is to do *pro bono* work to help build up your resume with some solid experience. A good road into this is working with an artist who is not yet big enough to be able to afford paid security and documenting your efforts by letters of endorsement and recommendation.

Chapter 6

THE WORLD OF FILM

While there are a lot of similarities between working with musicians and working with actresses and actors, there remain some very distinct differences. Just as our duties as bodyguards are different in the recording studio than while on tour, we need to look at the main elements in the world of movies to understand what our roles are in that arena and to be aware of the potential challenges. This world primarily revolves around studio shoots, on-location shoots, press junkets, and the ever-present award shows. Add to that the day-to-day activities of the actor or actress, and you can see how busy we can end up in this particular niche of the celebrity sector.

STUDIO SHOOTS

Before a film makes it to the big screen or a sitcom enters your home, it has to be created, some, or all, of that process occurs during studio shoots. In fact, in terms of our role, the protocols for us are very similar to the recording process on the music side. Musicians go in the sound booth to record, while actors go to the set to shoot.

A good example of studio shoots would be to imagine one of your favorite sitcoms. Notice how on a show like *Friends,* a big portion of it takes place in the same house? The studio set is usually an enclosed space with mockups of the environment where the scene is shot. Additionally, a vast majority of sci-fi films take place in the studio, because they use green screen extensively. (*Green screen* refers to the background behind the human actors that gets filtered with digital environments or effects added later.)

Consider the major studios such as Fox, Sony, or Warner Brothers: because of the sheer amount of people that come and go, the type of talent on set, and the types of equipment and machinery they invest in, the major studios usually have some pretty significant in-house security procedures already in place. That means that, much like in music recording, once we get our principal to the studio, we can then fade into the shadows. The challenge is figuring out how to do that while still maintaining situational awareness and not losing your edge.

Speaking of challenges, there's one that may seem humorous but can still be a real struggle to some nonetheless. On a movie set, you will find that the producers go out of their way to try to make sure that everybody is well-fed. They do this through a department called Craft Services. Keep in mind that this is done not out of the kindness of their heart, but rather practicality and efficiency. Imagine if everyone disappeared to go to Subway or Burger King at random times during the filming of a multimillion-dollar blockbuster. That's a lot of very valuable time wasted, and in film and television, time really is money. Instead, they bring the food and drink to you via catering, making it available pretty much around the clock.

Craft Services is like having a supermarket in your living room with everything you can think of at your disposal: doughnuts, cookies, cakes, candy, pizza, hotdogs, hamburgers, sodas, energy drinks, and the list goes on. You might notice that most of the items I named have high amounts of one of two main components, namely sugar or caffeine, and in many cases, both. The reason is simple: filming involves long days and nights, and they want to keep cast and crew alert and wired up.

So, while there is nothing to say that you can't partake of this sugary wonderland, you may want to think about how that single doughnut at noon combines with the three cupcakes that evening and the chocolate bar that night. Of course, shooting might last into the wee hours of the morning, so bring on the pizza and energy drinks. You can get away with loading up on these for a couple of days, but what if the shoot lasts a month? If you are not careful, you could walk away from a movie shoot 30 pounds heavier than when you started.

Another side effect of all that sugar and caffeine is that, after an initial energy burst, there's a crash that follows. If that happens when you still have five hours to go, you could end up trapped in a vicious cycle, where you have to load up even more just to stay awake. Maintaining discipline and not falling victim to small temptations that could have long-term consequences is the name of the game.

LOCATION SHOOTS

On-location shoots are often the opposite of the sterile environment we described in the section above. Just like touring on the music side, this is the part where a protector operating in the entertainment sector is really going to earn his or her paycheck. These location shoots can be very challenging, particularly if you're working with a highly recognizable VIP. Remember, you are not in the controlled environment of a studio; you are out shooting somewhere in the real world, and with that come real-world challenges.

So just think about if you were Will Smith and you were shooting *I Am Legend.* Scenes of the movie were shot in New York's Times Square. In this case, they digitally removed all the bystanders from the shots, but those people were very much there at the time he was shooting. As you can imagine, with Mr. Smith's star power, many of those fans and others would have loved to get up close and personal with the actor.

Even more extreme, consider if you were involved in *The Fast and The Furious,* where portions were shot in the Favelas in Brazil. That particular region has a host of security challenges, and who do you think it will fall to when it comes time to assist in navigating them?

For one, you need permission to enter a neighborhood such as the Favelas. I can personally attest to a situation like this when I took a client to Hatti. We didn't get the green light to visit some of the rougher neighborhoods from law enforcement; instead, permission came from a regional "spokesman," if you understand my meaning. It's only with his blessing that you have any assurance that the filming can continue unmolested. This aspect of the profession should be handled carefully, and if anything seems over your head, remember that a wise man brings in wiser men to assist.

AWARD SHOWS

Awards shows can make or break an entertainer. For instance, winning an Oscar or an Emmy can be the difference between starring in next summer's blockbuster or being relegated to late-night repeats with On Demand Cable.

With the importance placed on awards, the shows themselves become a gathering place for celebrities to see and be seen. Incidentally, the awards shows are also where you can shine as a protector. Some make it through the night on a wing and a prayer, and if the stars are in alignment, nothing too terrible goes wrong, but for those protectors who know how to function in that space by doing enough, but not too much, the phone will continue to ring time and again. The opportunities can also lead to a branching tree of networking, so the protector who excels could receive not just calls to work other shows, but also be noticed by decision-makers in attendance. These decision-makers will see how you conduct yourself in that environment and may want to use you on their future close protection assignments.

CHALLENGES

Tedious Times

As mentioned earlier, making films can be extremely tedious; while on set, you may hear "Take 1" eventually become "Take 100." The challenge to the protector will be to stay focused in an environment built on repetition. While it might not seem like much, I can guarantee you, based on Murphy's Law, that the minute you drop your focus and decide you're going to take a stroll down the hall, that's when something unfortunate happens.

Many Different Personalities and Bosses

A film set contains many moving parts, including people, each with their own personality, title, and degree of authority. At any given time, you could come into interaction on set with the director, the assistant director, the client, or the client's manager—and when you think about it, in a sense, all of these individuals could be considered your boss. Let's say you are providing security for an actor, and he says, "I'm getting ready to go in my trailer to take a thirty-minute nap before my next scene. Please don't let me be disturbed." You're sitting in front of the trailer, and about ten minutes go by when you see a male approach with no visible credentials. He's wearing an ill-fitting suit, with tie pulled loose, and he's got two small children with him. You observe the man as he starts beelining right for the door of the trailer. What do you do?

If your response is, "Excuse me sir, may I help you?", it's possible his reply may be, "You can't help me with anything. This is my movie."

Think about it: even if you know the director of the movie, would you know all six of the producers, who put up millions of dollars to get the project funded? If this individual is indeed who he says he is, one misstep on your part and he might make life difficult for the protectee. It should go without saying that it would also lead to some negative repercussions for you.

Whatever conversation or approach you take, my suggestion is to make sure you have it figured out before he reaches the door. Therefore, when you see him making that beeline to the trailer, it's time for you to step up and let loose with, not the physical, but the verbal judo to get the situation sorted out. If he's already reaching for the door and you decide to simply knock his hand away, as mentioned, the ramifications could be huge.

One approach: "Sir, just give me a couple of minutes. I'm going to try and see if I can sort this out." Don't have that conversation right at the door, because if he refuses to listen to reason right away, and instead begins to get loud, that might draw your protectee to the sound of the commotion, the very thing you were trying to avoid.

On a movie set, everybody thinks their job is ultra-important, and in some cases, they are correct. If you find yourself in the middle of these sensitive personalities, it's best to let diplomacy rule the day. Don't take things personally; just remember what your primary responsibility is, namely to protect your client and your client's image.

Long Periods Away From Family

Traveling can be exciting and rewarding, but there are serious downsides as well. The hours, days, and weeks can add up, and be it domestic or international, the stress can be overwhelming. The reality is, if you've been doing it long enough, at some point or another, you have likely hit a wall or two, which in turn, opens the door to mistakes. As amazing as most of us think we are, we are not superhuman nor infallible, and the pace of the business can take its toll. If we are not careful, it's highly possible to crash physically, emotionally, mentally, or even worse—all three.

Symptoms that may indicate the beginning of a downward spiral include tiredness, irritability, anger, anxiety, stomach pains, chest pains, and lack of sleep.

Every time this happens, it's wearing down your resilience and slowing your ability to recover. The cumulative effect can result in lasting depression and/or anxiety. In law enforcement circles, the feeling is generally called, "burnout," manifesting itself as any of the following:

- Excessive stress
- Fatigue
- Insomnia
- A negative spillover into personal relationships or home life
- Depression
- Anxiety
- Alcohol or substance abuse
- Heart disease
- High cholesterol
- Type 2 diabetes
- Stroke
- Obesity
- Vulnerability to illnesses

Depression and anxiety can cost you jobs, opportunities, relationships, and marriages. Sometimes we may not feel all of the negative effects while on the road, but those can still hit us hard shortly after our return home. For some, being home can be bittersweet; however, once there, now comes a longing for the camaraderie, brotherhood, and support that existed while on assignment. A bond that was created from the common goal of the mission and the shared vested success is now replaced with what some may consider the mundane.

At home, we may feel a lack of purpose, direction, or usefulness that we were getting from being a part of a tour family. You can feel isolated even among friends and family, who may have difficultly relating to—or even feel jealousy at—your life of travel and adventure on the road. They don't understand the downside in the form of sacrifices, and instead focus solely on the highlight reel.

There is also a rebounding effect to experiencing long stretches away from home and then suddenly long periods back without work while waiting on the next assignment. We sometimes may feel detached and out of touch with our home lives, and find ourselves missing the big functions, events, and logistical challenges that were previously defining our day-to-day activities.

Depression and anxiety are rampant in this tour life. We often don't know exactly what our schedule will be or when we're leaving next, whether tour dates will suddenly be extended, or worse, cancelled. When it's good—it's great, and when it's not, it's rough.[1]

For example, if you were providing security to the cast of the blockbuster film, *The Lord of the Rings,* not only were you in New Zealand filming for 274 days, but depending on where you reside, that could literally be the other side of the world. It's daytime there and you want to speak with your children, but you can't, because they are sleeping. It's been a long night for you and you are missing family, but your wife can't come to the phone because she's busy at work. Throw in the expenses involved with international calls and the hassle of intermittent or slow Wi-Fi, and you could see how long trips can bring some stress into your relationships.

Safety and Security Compromises

In this day of digital special effects wizardry, you might find it odd that an A-list actor like Tom Cruise puts himself in harm's way to do his own stunts when working on a film, but it has been publicly documented on many occasions. So, if you saw *Mission Impossible II* and recall the scene where Mr. Cruise was climbing a mountain, just know that wasn't a stunt double. The reason why some actors like to do their own stunts is that the camera can pull up tight, adding to the film's sense of realism.

However, that added realism has a somewhat different effect on us in our profession, and much as we would want to yell, "Cut!" and send in the stunt double, unfortunately, it's not our call.

Here is a classic case of how there can be reduced control over safety and security if they are perceived to compromise filming. Of course, the director wants that amazing shot of Tom Cruise hanging

---

1. George, Ryan. (2017, January 17). The Mental Health of Tour Life, on and off the Road. *This Tour Life.*

off the side of a mountain, as he's going to get a fantastic scene out of this. So, the protectee scales the side of the cliff, and you watch from 20 feet below, holding your breath. That's show business.

So how do you balance your responsibility to your client with the demands of the filmmakers (and sometimes, the client) to take risks for the benefit of the project? Do you just sit back and remain hands-off? Would they even be receptive to your concerns, or would they feel like you're interfering with the process?

To be successful, you need to first know what you are talking about, meaning having a clear understanding of the risk as well as an understanding of the safeguards in place. You next need to have the VIP's handlers (the management or talent agent) on your side. They need to have faith in your expertise and believe that you know what you're talking about, and this needs to take place *before* an incident occurs.

One thing you can do is use previous examples of on-set risk to VIPs that have caused harm. Unfortunately, there are several of these incidents that can be pulled from real life to help make your case.

Movie or martial arts aficionados might recall Brandon Lee, son of the legendary Bruce Lee, who was also the star of a budding film franchise called *The Crow*. While participating in his own stunt involving a firearm, a projectile shot out of the muzzle, striking Brandon and leading to his death. Tragic? Yes. Freak occurrence? Yes. Could you as a protector have played a role in preventing that tragedy on a movie set? In my opinion, yes.

I like to say that we can't outsource our responsibilities. Therefore, if there is anything that involves a real weapon or a convincing facsimile, I personally am going to inject myself into the process to check it out. In the case of a firearm, I am going to want to feel confident that the weapon is clear before it's used in a scene with my client. However, you should be aware that this argument could be a tough one to have with a director who has a film to complete. The same goes with the stunt coordinator, who naturally would feel like this is his world, and you are an outsider intruding in it. Here is where the strategy of utilizing your team, aka the client's handlers consisting of managers and agents, starts to pay dividends. When they respect your professional opinion and you can articulate your concerns, they can fight the battle for you.

From my own experience, I once had a client who starred in a movie where the scene called for him to be shot by a mobster, and of course, my red flag went up. Having read the script ahead of time, I knew the scene was coming, and once I discovered that the protectee, not a stunt double, was in the shot, I put my plan into action. I remember having the conversation with the director about how I needed to clear the weapons before they got on the set and receiving pushback in the form of, "We've got a stunt director and a prop master, so everything is taken care of."

I said, "Respectfully, I'm still going to need to clear the weapons before they are pointed at my client." At that point the director could be described as a combination of flustered and annoyed; remember, time is money in the world of film. He then took that gripe to the client's talent agent, whose response was, "Yes, Elijah needs to clear the weapons before the scene starts." Mission accomplished; however, in my mind, the only way I was able to be successful in this was due to the prior conversations I'd had with the talent agent and management in advance, using real-world examples.

While not everyone will succeed with this approach, these are the steps that separate the bodyguard who just stands at the door and reacts, from the proactive security specialist. It strikes a contrast in the overall level of protection that you give your client, and that difference will be noticed and, ultimately, appreciated.

Using another example, several years back, I traveled with a client to Italy, where he was shooting the cover of Italian *Vogue*. Having taken the protectee to his green room (the traditional name for a VIP's waiting area), I stood nearby while the art director explained the theme of the shoot. He went into vivid detail about how they were going to frame this beautiful shot, with the client standing on a castle bridge and the sun setting behind him, capturing the orange glow and blue sky. He ended the description by mentioning that flanking him on his left and right were going to be two majestic black panthers.

Upon hearing that, I figured they were going to shoot the photo with the client, take him away, and then bring the panthers out, shoot them, and finally photocompose them together. However, I soon found out that's not what they had in mind. Instead, the intention was to have the VIP on location and in frame with the panthers right next to him. As soon as the opportunity presented itself, I spoke to all the powers that be about the potential risks associated with this and, making a long story short, in the end, I was overruled.

So, when I say that you may have reduced control over safety and security if it compromises filming, or in this case, photography, I am speaking from firsthand experience, and letting you know it won't always end how you want it to.

A humorous postscript to this story is that once I realized that this was going to happen one way or the other, I met with the animal handlers at length. While speaking to them, they explained the training that these big cats go through. It turns out the panthers have been in many different movies and have had zero incidents. "Great," I say, "so if the cats do something, you have your firearm on standby, right?"

"Well, no."

"Then, you've got a tranquilizer gun, which will fire a dart delivering a sedative to knock them out, right?"

"Nope."

"Well, that just must be because your whip is effective enough to get the job done, right?"

"Again, no, we don't use a whip."

The trainer then informed me that if either of the cats decided to do something, by the time anyone could react, it would already be too late. Again, not a situation I'd ever willingly put a client in, and I did my best to raise my concerns to the powers that be regarding the potential safety issues. Ultimately, this discussion should be had even if your objections are overruled. Also, I didn't give up after the negative response; instead, I followed up with the trainers to see if I could mitigate the risk somehow. They allowed me to spend some time with the panthers before the protectee was brought to set. The trainer went over the commands, and I got to observe the animals at length and in close proximity. In the end, the shoot went off without a hitch, and one of the cats and I even became pretty good friends.

FILM RESOURCES

Like the music industry, the film industry has its own resources that you can target in your marketing efforts to work in this subsegment of the celebrity protection arena. These are the individuals and entities you need to reach out to in the worlds of television and feature films.

Then, once identified, it's lights, camera, action on your part to seal the deal.

The Talent Agency

The talent agency is much like the management agency for musicians. They're the people responsible for guiding the client's career. The difference is that talent agencies aren't solo operations; they usually represent dozens of actors and actresses worldwide. Some of the big ones, such as Creative Artist Agency (CAA), International Creative Management (ICM), and The William Morris Agency have massive A-List rosters across all genres. These are the company names that you should become familiar with if your interest is work in the world of film and television. For those who commit to doing the legwork, finding out which actors are represented by which agency isn't hard, as all are in the business of promoting their firms and highlighting their talent.

The Movie Studio

Movie studios are to the film industry what record companies are to the music industry. Think names like 21st Century Fox, Sony Pictures, or Warner Brothers. Like the record labels, these are massive companies with a multitude of layers, departments, red tape, and legal requirements. Candidly speaking, the odds are that, unless you are already firmly established, you are not usually going to be in a position to work directly with a studio.

A much better approach is to identify security agencies that already have working relationships with these studios and make yourself known to them. They have already gone through the lengthy vetting process, cut through the legal red tape, and established the proper connections. Explain to them who you are, what you can do, and what you can bring to the table.

Production Companies

A lot of people think that if you want to work in the film industry, you have to live in either New York City or Los Angeles. However, the reality is that motion pictures and television series shoot all over the globe. When a studio is making a movie in LA, and needs a scene that takes place at the St. Louis Arch and surrounding areas, are they going to pack everything up and fly the entire crew to Missouri, including caterers, wardrobe seamstresses, makeup technicians, and so forth? Negative.

Instead, they are going to hire a local production company in that region to provide as many of the components as possible without jeopardizing the quality of the shoot. If that's their philosophy for hair and makeup, you can imagine that many films also take the same approach to security. This is why, almost no matter where you are, you will find one or more local film production companies established there.

So even if you reside in an off-brand city or state, I would recommend identifying and tracking these local companies down and making them aware of who you are and what you do. You want to be in their Rolodex now, because later when a movie comes to your town, you want to be the first person that they call.

Keep in mind, this discussion is not about providing uniformed security. While there is often a need for that to safeguard the location and the equipment, there can also be a need for VIP protection, be it for an individual actor or just overseeing the entire production as a whole.

By example, for 15 years, I was based out of Minneapolis, Minnesota, where at one time, a large number of movies were shot because of the very attractive tax breaks the state offered as an incentive. With this is mind, I joined the Minnesota film board for a whopping $75 a year. Prior to me joining, there were three other security companies who were members of the film board: two were uniformed companies, and the third was a company consisting of retired motorcycle police officers. That last company had a unique selling point, in which they advertised their use of motorcycles to block off the streets during filming. Incidentally, I thought that was an ingenious business model—another example of developing a niche that makes you stand out.

However, they were not the only ones who stood out, as I had something different from all three. None of them had the experience or documented training in doing close protection one-on-one with VIPs, or if they did, they failed to put it front and center. So, when a large film was to come into town and contacted the film board for local resources, if anything had to do with security for the talent, the calls went to us almost every time.

These service relationships also extended beyond the actual shoot, so when the talent wanted to venture out into town, they now had someone with them who knew the area and looked the part. Additionally, they understood that privacy issues were not a concern, because the level of professionalism they were getting exceeded traditional guard services.

PRACTICAL ISSUES AND TECHNIQUES

Profile of a Celebrity

While everyone is different, celebrity clients often share similar traits. Identifying these traits before you start working with them will save you a lot of headaches in the long run. For one, you will have a better feel for why they act the way they do, giving you essentially your own guidebook on how to best approach and work with them—or alternatively, letting it serve as a flashing warning sign to you to stay away.

Narcissism

If we begin by building a profile of the prospective clients, one of the first things that we must acknowledge about celebrities is that by and large they are self-centered. I would imagine around ninety percent of celebrities could likely be professionally diagnosed as having narcissistic personalities. None of this description is designed to be viewed as a negative criticism; in fact, it's my belief that this is a component that gives them the drive that separates them from the pack. Words have meaning, so look at the vocabulary we use when describing them: we call them stars. That's not a coincidence when you think about it; the sun is the star at the center of the solar system, and everything revolves around it. Similar things can be said about celebrities and their entourages.

Understanding this aspect of the celebrity personality gives you some insight as to what may seem like a lack of empathy from them. This type of client might not care how you're feeling today. They may not remember that your birthday is quickly approaching. They might not seem concerned that you have a sick child at home.

I've had clients whom I've worked with for years. I don't miss acknowledging *their* birthdays, their spouse's birthdays, Christmas, and other special occasions. However, that same thoughtfulness is not necessarily reciprocated, and we won't even get into the number of times that I've worked for them on my birthday. If these perceived slights are something that will hurt your feelings, the reality of it is that protecting celebrities may not be the best avenue for you to pursue.

Contrast celebrities with corporate executives, where the responses may be a little more along the lines of what you would normally expect. If you ask them how their kids are doing, they'll tell you, and then in the majority of instances, inquire about yours, and so on. The reason is that most successful business people have an understanding of business and social norms. Somebody asks how you're doing, and you ask how they're doing; from an etiquette point of view, it's the correct thing to do.

The goal here is to better understand this segment of the market, namely celebrities who don't adhere to conventional norms. This is not passing judgement, as we should all value them as clients and work hard to provide exceptional service regardless of their idiosyncrasies.

Some might read this and say that the protection of celebrities is just too much of a handful, with too little appreciation. However, even if your area of interest is more corporate or political, in this day and age you are still likely to encounter celebrities while on the job. Rest assured that the corporate security teams of Google and Best Buy interact with the mega-stars of the entertainment world, be it at an in-store autograph signing or a visit to the corporate headquarters as a way of saying thank you for promoting their product. Therefore, an understanding of how the celebrity client thinks will help you accomplish your task more effectively.

Schedules and the Celebrity Client

Celebrity clients have hectic work and travel schedules, and that means that we are also going to have hectic work and travel schedules, because we go where they go.

So, if you are looking for a 9-5 kind of job, this is not the segment of the marketplace that you want to be in. If you are used to planning things out so that on the 30th of every month, you're going to take the kids to the water park, and then take your spouse out to a romantic candlelight dinner, this aspect of the industry is going to be tough.

Refer back to the dominant personality trait—most of the time, that VIP client is just not thinking that your wedding anniversary is right around the corner or that your 20-year high school reunion is next weekend if they have something major going on (and it's their definition of "major," not yours, that counts). The unwritten rule is that when you take them on as a client, their schedule becomes your schedule.

Now if they had something scheduled and it conflicted with something major in your personal life, most reasonable clients would allow you to take that time off; however, do keep in mind that the possibility exists that you might not get that phone call the next time there is a service need. Think about it: if you are not there this time, there will be someone else in your role, someone else who can do the job, and if they happen to perform exceptionally well and their schedule appears to be more accommodating, that can sometimes create problems for you.

Again, we are faced with the fact that, while not fair, it's a reality of the marketplace with this client type that protectors need to be aware of. My suggestion is to have scheduled time off negotiated into the contract from its outset so that it is clear in black-and-white. It's also a good practice to give the client notice of your scheduled time off and, if possible, to fill the open position with someone in your personal network whom you trust.

The Celebrity Performance Schedule

A longtime associate of mine used to work for one of the biggest names in pop music. I recall the occasion, which some might say was an act of luck, where he was hired on the spot right when the VIP was an emerging star with a very catchy record. Shortly afterwards, the client scored one of the biggest records of his career, went on tour, and rose to monumental success. The interesting thing about this story is that once out, this particular VIP stayed on the road touring for practically three years straight. Of course, that meant that his protector also toured for that same period. While everyone would envy that portfolio of consistent business, it's important to also keep in mind the flip side of the coin. During those three years, that protector was home for a total of about two months. With a family, that meant that the agent saw his wife and kids about 60 days, *nonconsecutive* days, out of more than a thousand.

Of course, there was a nice paycheck associated with the assignment, but can you imagine the stresses on family life that come with that kind of travel schedule? It's great to earn well and travel the world, but we have to factor in the reality of what happens when our time is not our own. What happens when you don't get to take advantage of those things that you work hard for? What happens when you're providing for your family, but you can't be there for your family? Protecting celebrities can be extremely rewarding; however, like most things in life, those rewards come because of what you have to trade for them.

Instant Fame

We've all heard the stories of people who come suddenly into a huge amount of money or notoriety and they have no idea how to deal with it. Even well-adjusted people would have a hard time, but for sure, overnight success can produce some bad behaviors.

We've also all read story after story about celebrities acting out, and when you're the one protecting them, you may actually witness this firsthand. When you learn of a celebrity getting in trouble in the public eye, you always hear someone say, "If *I* had that kind of money, I'd still be my regular self." While I think everyone wishes that were true, more often than not, that kind of money and fame can lead to problems for anyone, especially when it comes virtually overnight.

Think about it: if on Monday you were an average Joe, barely making ends meet, but by Friday you've become a multimillionaire, with hundreds of thousands of fans watching your every move, that type of instant success can be hard to cope with. Or how about the kid from below the poverty line who never felt appreciated and now, because of his jump shot or singing voice, is quickly surrounded by people who basically tell him that he's the best thing to ever arrive on planet Earth. Statistically speaking, the ones who *don't* act out in these situations are probably the exceptions to the rule.

Unfortunately, when these celebrities do act out they tend to leave a mess behind them, and someone has to clean it up. That's a tricky spot to be in, and my advice is to instead try and be the person who directly or indirectly helps them avoid the mess in the first place.

For the untrained protector, that is a lot easier said than done. In fact, all too many times when I hear about celebrities doing something bad enough that it gets reported in the media, there is also a bodyguard involved. When I dig deeper into the story, the protector usually turns out to have been trying to get the client out of a mess but didn't do it correctly. Oftentimes, those situations may have been beyond the bodyguard's control, but it doesn't really matter, as it's the same end result. We have to be prepared to either help the protectees help themselves or know when to step away if we come to the realization that they are on a path to self-destruction.

Not in the Job Description

Celebrities are also much more likely to ask bodyguards to perform duties outside of their normal job requirements. This can range from seemingly innocuous tasks, like asking you to carry the groceries, to requests that are problematic or even potentially illegal. Let me go on record and say this: if your client is asking you to do something illegal, you should NOT be working for them; that road usually ends at a very bad place.

Some requests that could seem to be unreasonable could all come down to a matter of perception. For example, should bodyguards be carrying bags for clients? When I pose this to students in my training courses, that's a question that usually divides the room fairly equally. Some are of the position that, as we work for the client, it's a service-based industry, and if they ask us to do something within reason, why not? The counter to that is that, as protectors, we need our hands free to respond to potential threats. What if we need to respond to an attacker, but our hands are full of suitcases or grocery bags?

I once had a celebrity client on the roster who, as part of her show, would perform in these big, extravagant gowns. Far from ordinary dresses, these were elaborate, one-of-a-kind, and not cheap. When she travelled for a performance, the dresses of course came with us in several large garment cases. On a past occasion, the airline had lost some of her luggage, causing her to be ultra-sensitive to the cases being separated from us while traveling. In light of that, the protectee wanted to minimize the baggage being out of our sight as much as possible, with that also extending to our arrivals at hotels. Traditionally, an arrival to a hotel involves pulling up and immediately escorting the VIP to the elevator and to the room, leaving the luggage to the bellman. However, with this particular client, her wishes were for the bags to also go with us. So, in this scenario, do we, the bodyguards, carry the bags?

Let's take a moment to think about what the client really wants: it's not that she wants us to personally pick up the bags and carry them ourselves just to make sure that all those hours in the gym don't go to waste. What the client actually is looking for is for someone reliable to facilitate getting something she cares about from point A to point B. The savvy protector understands that being a facilitator is one of our primary roles. Our job is to make sure that objectives get completed to the client's satisfaction—without compromising his or her security.

In essence, you don't need to necessarily carry the bags yourself, because moving the VIP from the car to the hotel and up to the room is the top priority; instead, all you need to do is manage the situation. Now, if you're going to move the VIP up to the room, but you know that she doesn't want the bag to be out of your presence, why not put in a phone call ahead of time to the hotel to make arrangements?

In this scenario, I would explain to the hotel precisely what I want them to do, because if you don't, they will do what their protocol is. Traditionally with luxury hotels, they'll get the luggage, take it out of the public space, and head up the back elevator. Unfortunately, that system means it ends up where you can't keep an eye on it, which means the client's wishes are not being met. A simple adjustment to their protocol, in this case having them meet you with the bell cart and instructing them that they will be moving directly behind you and traveling in the same elevator, solves the problem. With that said, the time to have that discussion is not when you pull up outside the hotel entrance. We don't want the protectee to be exposed, essentially sitting on the "X," while we're in an involved discussion with the bellboy. Remember, the client just wants their requests handled—how you handle it is usually up to you. Ultimately, you just need to balance their requests with their safety and security.

Who Gets the Coffee?

Imagine you're in a foreign country, positioned outside your client's hotel room door in anticipation of a movement occurring that morning. The protectee opens the door, dressed only in a robe, and in a groggy voice that all but assures he's going to be late, says, "I need a double mocha decaf cappuccino." And then promptly shuts the door. What do you do?

Some protectors will snap to it, dashing out to the closest Starbucks or local equivalent to find the beverage. It was the client's request, after all, and up to this point it's been an uneventful trip. However, it's times like that when Murphy's Law strikes. That's when the fire alarm is pulled, and you walk back up to find the hotel evacuated, with your protectee nowhere in sight. Remember, as with the luggage, the client doesn't necessarily want *you* to go and get coffee. The client simply wants the next knock on the door to be you with coffee in your hand.

Some bodyguards get too focused on the customer service aspect, and that creates some big gaps in protection. This is why it's important to foster good relationships wherever you go, so that you can delegate the client's needs. The misconception is that bodyguards are there only for bullet-blocking and dropkicks, but oftentimes it's just about making sure the client gets through their day with as little intrusion as possible. To do that takes problem-solving, an understanding of logistics, verbal judo, and the previously-mentioned delegation skills. If you can master these tactics, along with the exciting stuff, your phone will continue to ring, and you can carve out a long-term career in this industry.

Celebrity and Accessibility

I'd hazard a guess that most of the people who find themselves no longer working in the celebrity protection field did something wrong in their interactions with either the crowds, the fans, or the media. When it comes down to it, the biggest challenge we have to figure out as protectors is how to balance celebrity and the challenges of accessibility. Much as they might protest otherwise, celebrities can't exist in splendid isolation. A big part of their lives requires interacting with those three entities, and if that's in *their* job description, it also becomes part of ours.

Celebrities can't keep their fans if they don't engage with them, and with the aforementioned emergence of streaming services and digital piracy, music and movies aren't selling like they did in the past. To counter that, entertainers have to find new ways to interact with their adoring public so that they will continue to support them and buy their product.

That notwithstanding, in our role it's important for us to create barriers, physical and otherwise, to manage risk. We have to operate from a mindset of keeping the fans and others back so they don't intentionally or unintentionally cause harm to the VIP. This dance between all three parties (the protectee, the protector, and the public) is a symbiotic relationship; however, if the scales are tipped too much in any direction, the headaches multiply exponentially.

THE ADVANCE SURVEY

For most people, our home gives us the best sense of safety, security, and refuge, with arguably the second being the office, which is essentially home away from home. Contrasting that, the time when a VIP is most at risk is while in transit, with a close runner up being the occasions when they are required to enter unfamiliar places. As such, we have to understand the exposure a celebrity who tours the world faces, appearing at various venues in different cities and countries, at times on a nightly basis. It is the responsibility of the advance agent to survey a site and make all necessary arrangements. This includes routes, times, and mode of travel. The survey covers everything that will in any way impact the security of the VIP and prepare for contingencies. A sample of a proven advance survey form checklist is found in Appendix A of this book.

A summary of the things a security agent must do and know would be reflected in three primary categories: anticipation, planning, and preparation.

ANTICIPATE

You need to anticipate anything that could, would, or might happen to endanger the safety of the transiting protectee. And you need to do everything you can do to prevent anything from happening to endanger the person protected.

PLAN

You need to plan:

- The itinerary, with primary and alternate routes, times of arrivals and departures.
- The method and means of providing transportation.
- Emergency contingencies.

PREPARE

Visit each site, drive each route, and learn ALL there is to know about the immediate environment, alternate routes, escape contingencies, alleys, emergency facilities, and so forth. And prepare the vehicles as follows: Maintain, Fuel, Inspect, and Search.[2]

What does the advance agent need to know? The short answer is, they need to know everything. They must have contingency plans for any imaginable scenario that may (and certainly will) suddenly present itself. It could be anything from an electrical failure, to sudden illness, to responding to a flat tire on the client's car. The advance agent must know everything about the venue, forum, or event that the VIP will be attending and have a plan on what to do if something goes wrong.

As protectors, we always want to move from the known to the known. We want to know as much as possible about where we're going before we bring the protectee into that environment so that we can minimize the risks to our client.

The key to conducting stellar advances is a superior grasp on logistics. If you understand how point A is interconnected with points B and C, you have the basics. However, those who make a name for themselves in this area usually possess great attention to detail and are well organized. I've seen agents who might have otherwise gone unnoticed for protective assignments get placed on the team because they were above average in their understanding and execution of advances. This can even lead to its own revenue stream, as there are individuals who specialize in doing advances for hire for other teams on a contractual basis.

---

2. June, Dale L (2015). *Introduction to Executive Protection* (3rd ed.). Boca Raton: CRC Press.

CLONING THE PROTECTOR

Usually, the bodyguard would love an extra set of eyes, ears, and hands taking care of the site advance, because we have enough on our plates just keeping eyes on the client, particularly if they are high profile/high visibility. The dilemma for all in the profession is how to get a successful advance completed when we also need to be with the client. Essentially, we have to be in two places at once.

So, until cloning becomes the norm, the next best solution is assigning that task to a second person on your team. In addition to conducting the actual advance itself, you need that person to also be able to convey the information back to you clearly. The term I like to use is, "paint me a picture," meaning give it to me in such a way that, at a quick glance, I can see it's a tree, but if and when I have more time to study it, I would notice the color and texture of the leaves, if it was a willow or pine, etc. That is how we want the advance to come across, clear enough to be quickly understood, but also containing additional information that can be referred to if the agent in charge needs to drill down deeper.

If you have a larger team and the plan is to visit (or potentially visit) multiple locations, you might send one agent to one site, and one to another. Alternatively, you might have one dedicated agent leap-frogging from one site to the next, advancing each ahead of your arrival.

Let's say your client has a performance scheduled in a different city; while still at the hotel with the protectee, you send your advance agent to the concert venue to do the advance there. After the concert, there's a paid night club appearance, so at some point during the show or directly afterwards you send him over to the club to do the advance at that site. While at the club, but prior to leaving, you send him outside to make sure the vehicle is squared away and things look kosher. Again, we try to always keep with the philosophy of moving from the known to the known.

SUBTLETY WINS

Just a reminder that most of this book has been about overt actions and activities, but a site advance is usually best done much more subtly. If you go to some locations and start asking unusual questions and are clearly poking around, you'll just be bringing more attention to your visit, when what you really want is to get in and out. Pulling out your phone and obviously (and obnoxiously) shooting video of the entrances and exits at a location is just asking for trouble. Much the same could be accomplished by just walking in like a normal customer and making mental notes while looking at the menu.

Now there will be some cases where there are restricted access areas, and you'll have to explain who you are to get access. Even then, try and do that subtly and respectfully, regardless of who the VIP is. Also avoid falling into the habit of ordering people around or demanding that they provide you information. As the saying goes, you'll catch more flies with honey than you will with vinegar.

In a post-9/11 world, we also have to be careful how the questions we ask are perceived, especially when working internationally, because some parts of the world can be super-sensitive to an unfamiliar person's motives. So, while it's great to get photographs and video to supplement your advance, there are some places where that can get you questioned or even arrested and detained.

SECURITY SURVEY

The initial act by the protective team upon being hired by a celebrity is to conduct a complete security survey of the lifestyle, business office, and home of the celebrity. There may be a previous survey done by a prior security team that the new team may use as a guide; however, a new survey must be conducted because new vulnerabilities may have developed or had been overlooked since the last. A physical survey looks into every aspect of the celebrity's environment. Findings and recommendations include static security posts, alarm systems and lighting, logs, policies, and procedures.

Protocols for visitors and staff include admission to the celebrity's home and office, the handling of deliveries and mail, security assignments, travel arrangements and vehicles, unique codes or passwords, contact numbers, and so forth.

The survey, complete with recommendations and procedures, must be documented and dated, kept confidential with a "need to know" designation, and approved by the client or a trusted designee. Only relevant portions should be shared with the actual protectee, and security standard operating procedures should not be shared outside the protective team. Generic examples of physical property survey checklists that can be adapted to particular circumstances are readily available on a number of online security websites using the keywords "physical security surveys" or "security checklists forms." A checklist is merely a tool to ensure that nothing is overlooked. They can be customized as needed for any particular location. A version of an inclusive checklist example is found at: http://www.isaca.org/Groups/Professional-English/physical-security/GroupDocuments/physical security.pdf

Chapter 7

VEHICLES

The majority of what we do as protectors involves moving our clients from point A to point B, and aside from walking, the next biggest mode of locomotion involves motor vehicles. Unfortunately, that also happens to be where the majority of attacks against protectees are known to take place. With that in mind, it is especially important to have a mastery of how to operate in and around the vehicle, as well as the vehicle itself, as it literally could be the difference between life and death.

ADVANCE PREPARATION

In a perfect world, we would always have an experienced trained security driver behind the wheel of any vehicle we put the protectee inside. Life, however, is not always perfect. That means that in some instances you will have a civilian driver, untrained in security issues, who's going to be responsible for what can most certainly be termed precious cargo. What that means is that you will have to take it upon yourself to educate the driver so that they understand at least a minimum of what you are going to need from them in their role. Yet before you can communicate this information to them, you have to know the process and the vehicle intimately yourself.

STANDARDS

In terms of what vehicle type you should choose to transport your client, 15 or 20 years ago, the classic black stretch limousines were the vehicle of choice for VIPs. However, from a practical sense, they were gas guzzlers, difficult to maneuver, and difficult to maintain and repair; in essence, they were more useful as a status symbol than anything else. These days, the vehicles most utilized are luxury SUVs, because they offer clients a bit more anonymity, combined with seating room and luggage space. As a result, you need to make yourself familiar with the main vehicles used in the US market: the Cadillac Escalade, the Chevy Suburban, and to a lesser extent, the Chevy Tahoe and the Lincoln Navigator.

When you go overseas, this setup changes dramatically. For instance, in the UK, they don't use larger SUVs at the frequency you see in the United States, opting instead for luxury vans or the more compact Range Rover or Mercedes G-Wagon. One factor for this is that the large vehicles never gained much popularity with consumers there due to the narrow city streets. Additionally, in some countries, such as Nigeria or Colombia, what is considered a luxury SUV is dramatically different from what you'd expect in North America. If you will be travelling abroad with your client, you have to take it upon yourself to research and become familiar with the best vehicles available in each destination.

SPECIALTY VEHICLES

When it comes to the luxury sedan category, the market leader is Mercedes Benz, which incidentally makes the Mercedes Maybach, a $350,000 ultra-luxury car with pretty much every bell and whistle you could think of (flame throwers optional).

Whether it's the Rolls Royce, where the doors open from the opposite direction, or the Porsche, where the battery is in the rear and the trunk is in the front, it's going to be difficult to learn the vehicle comprehensively if you first encounter it only at the same time your client does on assignment. What I would instead recommend is, as part of your ongoing professional development, take some time and visit a few local high-end dealerships in your area and have them demo the above-mentioned cars.

I understand: you might now be thinking that not only do you not have the funds to buy a Rolls Royce, once you tell them that, they are going to laugh you out of the dealership.

Here's an instance where a little bit of showmanship and verbal judo can work wonders: ditch the jeans and t-shirt and instead, throw on the power suit with a nice polish on the shoes. Once there, ask to speak to the manager, not the salesperson. Present your professional business card and explain that you own (or work for) an executive protection company. Explain how your clients include some high net-worth individuals and you're doing the initial evaluation of a vehicle for your protectee prior to their selection.

Chances are they are going to be happy to demo the car for you, because they ultimately want to forge a relationship with you if any of your clients decide to buy a vehicle in the future. Personally speaking, I can recall a time several years back where I had a client who ordered a Mercedes Maybach when they were first coming off the assembly line. Just prior to delivery, I had the dealer demo the car for me and, believe me, it was like learning how all the controls in an aircraft cockpit work. There was even an umbrella that pops out of the door when you press a certain lever. I suppose that, for that amount of money, it should!

Whatever the vehicle, you need to know what makes it tick, and if you have a civilian driver, you have to make sure he knows. You'd be surprised how many drivers have no idea about something as simple as disabling the overhead dome light when the door opens. You will want answers for questions from the basic to the exotic, like does the vehicle have a spare tire, how is it accessed, which side is the gas tank on, and is it a locking tank? These things may seem routine, but there may come a time when, in an emergency situation, knowing some of these things may make a crucial difference.

WHAT YOU NEED TO LEARN

Below is an abridged checklist of items you want to make sure you are familiar with in any vehicle your client will be traveling in.

Capacity

This is one of the reasons why your client chooses a luxury SUV versus using a sedan. It's important to gauge the level of comfort for the client in terms of space as well as plot out room for the luggage.

Yes, you could drive your client in a Porsche, but where are you going to put all the suitcases?

Lighting

Fog lights really are designed for fog, so fumbling around under the steering wheel when visibility conditions are low is never a good idea. Learn the lighting systems, both interior and exterior. Find out how to disable the overhead interior light coming on when the door is opened—at night, that light illuminates the cabin and exposes who and where the VIP is. Surprisingly, a large number of drivers don't know where the switch is to shut this feature off, but you should.

Radio

I know, I know, the radio is not your problem. That is, until your client leans forward and asks you to change the station, and you spend ten minutes figuring it out when you should be scanning the surroundings for trouble.

Temperature Control

Set the control to a comfortable position based off of the environment and leave it there. If the client wishes to make changes, they will notify you. While it may be uncomfortable for you, the reality is, only one vote counts when it comes to temperate control: the VIP's.

GPS

Working knowledge of that specific vehicle's GPS/map system can be critical, and not only for the obvious reasons that come to mind of getting from point A to point B. If you're renting a car for your client, and your driver programs the GPS, unless you actively take steps to clear that information, you're leaving a nice digital footprint for the nosy rental staff or next driver to see. I personally get in rentals all the time, and with a few button prompts can see the places the previous driver had visited and even presets like "home" or personal phone numbers that his or her phonebook has synced.

Door Locks

Sometimes, safety features are not your friend. Child locks are great for children, but for adults in the back seat, not so much. While, in a perfect world, we want to control all the doors, meaning that we open the door for the client to get in and out, VIPs don't want to feel like they are in prison, and the minute they push on the handle and nothing happens, they immediately feel like a 6-year-old on time-out. Save yourself the grief, and disengage the child locks in the beginning.

Seatbelts

You don't need the flight attendant to demonstrate how to buckle or unbuckle a seatbelt, but you do need to check how much tension there is in the belt and how much space it allows you. Chances are, you will be sitting in the car with a few "tools" on, and you don't want them to imprint or snag. Have you ever used a seatbelt cutting tool? Don't wait until you are in an accident. Find a junkyard, give the manager 20 bucks, and spend some time actually trying it.

Gas Tank

It's a no-brainer, but a full tank of gas is a requirement before you start any assignment. In my mind, the half tank mark is actually "empty," so whenever possible, top off. No one wants to leave their protectee at the restaurant while they run over to the gas station to fill up.

Tires

You can have the rarest, fastest, most exclusive car ever, but if the tires are lousy, or if you get a flat tire and don't know where that spare is, you're potentially endangering your client.

Fire Extinguisher and Medical Kits

A fire extinguisher and a well-provisioned emergency medical kit are necessary requisites in the vehicle you will be traveling in. These items should not be stored in the trunk, but in the passenger compartment for easy access in a time of need.

Flairs, Reflectors, and Jumper Cables

In an emergency (vehicle down) it is helpful to have flairs or reflectors to place in locations that will alert other drivers of a disabled vehicle. Additionally, as we all know, there is nothing worse or more embarrassing than finding out that the battery is dead on your mode of transportation when it's time to leave; a good set of jumper cables and knowing how to operate them is important.

Placement

In addition to the above, you also need to know where you exist in the space inside the car. Let's assume that you already have a driver behind the wheel; the optimal place for the protector inside the vehicle is the front right seat. The front passenger seat allows the protector to see what's going on, giving you the widest field of view of what's happening in the area. Sitting in the back with the client might technically make him or her easier to reach in an emergency; however, it's likely to also make him or her uncomfortable, and since they spend large chunks of their day in transit, comfort is important.

Ideally, I place the protectee behind me in the rear right seat, not behind the driver, so that when we come to a stop, I don't have to go all the way around the car to get to him. It allows for an efficiency of movement getting in and out of the vehicle; remember, we don't want to "sit on the X" any longer than we have to.

There's another, grimmer reason for not placing the protectee behind the driver. If a trained and motivated attacker wants to stop a vehicle, he does it by taking out the driver. If the client is behind the driver, the bullets aimed at the driver have an increased chance of also hitting the protectee.

While the same could be said of the front right seat, as it relates to the protection agent, we are admittedly not in the best place in terms of self-preservation, but of course we assume the responsibilities and risks that come with this job. This is where the case is made for body armor and secure route planning so that everyone, including us, gets home safe.

OIL STAINS AND BEING ON TIME

No need for a mechanic in this section: being oil stained in our industry does not refer to an engine problem, but rather a personal one: namely, tardiness. Being oil stained is when the client or the team is scheduled to depart at a certain time and a member of the detail is late. In some cases, allowances can be made, but if wheels-up is 10:00 and you get downstairs at 10:03, you might not see the vehicle, but instead a greasy black patch in the area where the SUV used to be. If you ever find yourself in that situation, take a good long look at that oil stain and use it as a reminder to be on time for each and every movement.

MOVING IN AND OUT OF CARS

Probably the most common movement that we have to facilitate is also one of the subtler ones; namely, the proper way to get the protectee in and out of the vehicle. Knowing that the majority of attacks occur in and around the vehicle, we have to be on heightened alert, keeping our head on a swivel at all times. This is the point where the attacker has the biggest window of opportunity to do something bad, and the unfortunate reality is as it relates to attacks, the bad guys get to choose the time and the place. To compensate for this disadvantage, we have to cheat, meaning that we have to use all the tools in our bag of tricks to tilt the scales back in our favor as much as possible.

When walking the protectee to the car, we as protectors are still responsible for 360 degrees of coverage, including what's behind us. The optimal position, which presents the widest field of view, is at the client's rear, positioned a bit to either side so that our view of what's ahead is not obstructed. However, as we get closer to the vehicle, we are going to want to open up the width and pace of our stride, passing the protectee, so as to get to the car door before he or she does. When this happens correctly, the client never has to break stride or come to a stop, and with practice the movement is seamless and fluid.

DOORS OPEN

Sometimes success means unlearning some things. Case in point, all our life we have been opening car doors pretty much the same way; usually, the action consists of gripping the door handle and pulling it. However, if you're holding the car door by the handle, and suddenly a loud noise occurs such as a gunshot, explosion, or even a car backfiring, the normal human response is to flinch. Yet when we do that, you end up with a handful of door handle, and not a handful of protectee.

So, in keeping with the mantra of cheating where we can, as we pull the door open, the most effective thing to do is immediately take our hand off the handle. We still need to make sure to maintain positive control of the door by grabbing the side of it so that it doesn't swing back and hit the client. As the protectee moves inside, we also need to be careful when closing the door, resisting the urge to rush the process more than we have to. Move too fast and the VIP's leg might not be in the car yet, and slamming will hurt not only them, but likely your career.

As we are placing the protectee inside the vehicle, we will want the lion's share of our attention to still be focused on observing what is going on outside the car; in all likelihood, if there is a threat, that's where it would emerge from. Once the protectee is inside, the vehicle is on the "X," so you want to also get inside (front right seat) so that the vehicle can get moving as quickly as possible. With practice and repetition, this becomes a naturally choreographed dance, with the VIP not even noticing all the thought that goes into it.

THE DRIVER'S ROLE

There's a saying in the close protection industry: drivers drive. What that means is that, ideally, we want the person behind the wheel to focus solely on getting the protectee safely to their destination. While most security-trained drivers can quickly adapt to that role, the reality is that in celebrity protection, the use of commercial car services and drivers is commonplace. This requires us to shift the thinking of the commercial drivers as their training can be at times contrary to our protocols.

For example, one of the first things a commercial car service driver wants to do when arriving at a destination is to jump out and open the door for the passengers in the back seat. That's what they are trained to do, and it is an ingrained part of the customer service experience in their industry.

When you work with a driver who isn't already part of your team, spend time delivering a briefing before you set out. Let him know that you will take care of the doors, and the temperature, and the radio; all you need him to do is stay alert and drive safely. Remember to do this in a way that doesn't hurt feelings or bruise egos; you don't want to create an issue where there wasn't one—you want him on your side and fully engaged. You want his head in the game, not annoyed from the start because some guy came out of nowhere, delivered all these orders, and made demands that ran contradictory to his training.

With that said, there are exceptions to that rule. Perhaps there's an occasion where the protectee has a family member with them in the vehicle. In those situations, I open the door for the client, and the other passenger slides over and comes out the same way. Sometimes, I may be with a client who has a high level of exposure, but the person that they are traveling with doesn't want to be seen getting out at the exact same time. In those cases, I take the protectee out of the car and we start moving, and then the other person gets out shortly after on their own steam. On those occasions if it's a member of the opposite sex, I rarely have a problem with the driver letting them out as a courtesy. Sometimes I reverse the order and let the other passenger get out first and go, so the paparazzi don't capture them together. In all of these cases, a number of factors are at play, such as the size of the team, the level of exposure we are looking to avoid, and the potential risks.

Another good tip is that, when you arrive at your destination and the vehicle comes to a stop, you may want to tell the driver to just keep his foot on the brake as opposed to putting it fully in Park. The reason is, most modern cars have a default feature that will unlock the doors when the vehicle is put in "P." In the event that feature is engaged, and you need to park, quickly lock the door again as a matter of protocol.

EMBUSSING AND DEBUSSING

At the point when you've arrived at your destination, you usually want to escort the protectee out of the vehicle quickly, spending as little time as possible on the "X." This is referred to as *debussing*.

As the protector, you exit the vehicle first, performing a scan of the area, and it is only when you are comfortable that you have the protectee exit. I recommend having a predetermined signal between you and the client so you both know when you are ready. Some agents tap on the vehicle door or window when they are ready for the VIP to exit. I, however, do not recommend this; considering the amount of time that you and your principal spend in transit, that could get very annoying in the long-term.

Alternatively, you could nod to them when you're ready, but it's likely you won't be able to see them nodding back due to the fact that the majority of luxury vehicle windows traditionally have strong window tinting.

One technique that I use is that, when I get out of the car, I move to the rear passenger's door and stand in front of it as I'm scanning. This gives me the added bonus of providing body coverage to the client's window. If I'm comfortable with the environment, I next crack the door slightly. When the client is ready to move, they apply light pressure to the door, which is my signal to open it fully and escort them out of the vehicle and to their destination. It's a choreography of movement that, when practiced, looks natural and effective.

The use of body coverage during the debus puts you between the potential threat and the VIP exiting the vehicle. It also has an added value when working with female clients; by positioning yourself correctly, you put yourself in between them and any photographers who might immediately begin snapping at a time when the client is not done applying their make up or adjusting their wardrobe. Make no doubt about it, the paparazzi would love to capture an embarrassing up-skirt photo and run with it all the way to the bank.

MOTORCADES

When most people think of a motorcade, the image that comes to mind is dignitary-level, such as how the President or other Heads of

State travel. However, by definition, a motorcade is simply a procession of two or more vehicles. So, if you have more than one vehicle traveling with you as you move your client, you have a motorcade.

Motorcades in a protective security detail are designed to swiftly and safely move the protectee, acting as mobile safe havens, and even as a means of providing camouflage at times. Yet with this additional layer of security also come additional layers of complexity. If you don't have the benefit of a security-trained driver, you may have to give a crash course (no pun intended) on what to expect.

In the private sector, barring any unusual circumstances, motorcades usually restrict themselves to two or three vehicles. Unless you are attending a special event, there is usually no authorized entity providing intersection and traffic control, such as local law enforcement blocking intersections for you, so that you can run through red traffic lights without stopping.

With or without the benefits of police traffic control, the important thing to remember is that the motorcade acts as one entity. That means the group should never be separated by traffic intersections or other vehicles. As such, driver attentiveness at all times is a must.

Whether you will have law enforcement resources available to you in your motorcade depends on a number of factors, such as the type of VIP you're working with, the level of their celebrity, the organization that invited you, etc. In almost all cases, I recommend that if you have law enforcement resources available and they offer you support, take it, as it will make your life easier. Most celebrities will happily accept a police escort, even if they say they don't like the police in their songs. The exception to this is if you want to remain off the radar, as a police escort will certainly get heads turning and draw attention.

Sometimes you can get police support free of charge, while other times you will have to pay out of the budget for it. It depends on your client, the event, and the amount of goodwill you have with the local police department.

Recalling one occasion, we landed at Chicago's O'Hare airport for a massive event in the downtown area. On any given day of the week, Chicago traffic can be notoriously bad, and knowing this, police traffic control was set up in advance. The officers met us at the airport in their squad cars, and it was lights and sirens all the way downtown to our destination; in fact, we spent approximately three-fourths of the trip driving on the shoulder of the road.

Distance between one car and the next is also important in motorcade operations. You don't want someone, knowingly or unwittingly, breaking into your motorcade, as your risk factor then increases. We counter this with the use of effective blocking, and to do so, the drivers need to be close enough so everyone in the motorcade can make the lights at the intersections, as well as not allow other vehicles to cut in. With that said, you don't want to be so close that, if a vehicle has to stop or brake quickly, the driver behind doesn't have time to react and runs into the car in front. Here is yet another case to be made for having a trained security driver behind the wheel.

CHOOSING A DRIVER

When choosing a driver, my first choice is to have a member of my team behind the wheel; the comfort of working with someone who has trained the same way and in the same system as you cannot be overstated. Barring that, my second choice is a driver who has a degree of experience working with VIPs and is certified for security driving. There are several excellent organizations that teach protective driving skills, such as Tony Scotti's Vehicle Dynamics Institute (VDI).

The third choice, which is sometimes the only choice available, is to utilize a commercial car service. For obvious reasons, this is less desirable than either of the first two, but sometimes we have to play the hand that we are dealt. When faced with this situation, apply all the due diligence that you can, and don't just accept any driver they send you. Make it a point to ask questions about his or her level of experience and demeanor. Also consider forming a strategic alliance with companies that you like so that they understand how you operate and will work to meet your needs in the future.

Of course, the important thing is to brief the actual driver who is going to be behind the wheel of your vehicle. Remember, you as the protector are introducing a big unknown into the protective equation, so it pays to be thorough. While the car service itself may have a long-standing reputation, you need to have a good feel for the person in the front left seat.

TOUR BUSES

Working with celebrities, particularly musicians for any length of time, you are likely going to encounter tour buses. Big, imposing, and in many cases, comfortable, you will have to think about how you need to modify your mobile protective operations, because the configuration is different on a number of levels than what you may be used to.

The typical tour bus is divided into three sections: there is the front cockpit, where the driver is, a lounge or living space usually consisting of seating, tables and audio/video equipment, and then there is the sleeping area. The sleeping area contains the bunks, ranging from four on some buses to as many as 12 on others. With a shorter bunk count, the rear of the bus can be converted into a master suite or an additional lounge. There are some buses that have outfitted this space into a fully functional recording studio on wheels. Regardless, I usually like to designate this area as the VIP's private space, giving them an area of refuge to retreat to.

For most US tour buses, there is only one door, meaning we don't have the convenience of multiple entry and exit points like in an SUV. With that said, all buses come equipped with emergency exits, traditionally in the form of a sealed window that can be pushed out in the event of an emergency. Make sure you get to know the location of each and how they operate. Due to the sole access point almost always being located in the front cabin up near the driver, the optimal position for the protector is the same as in an SUV: the front right seat.

From this vantage point, you get the widest field of view and also get to see who's coming on and exiting off the bus. Having an accurate passenger count is essential, as you don't want to inadvertently oil-stain a member of the entourage who went inside the gas station during a fuel stop. So not only is the tour bus a means of conveyance, you will also want to treat it like the protectee's residence, meaning that you will want to screen everyone entering, and also give the client some breathing room as you are in close quarters. The best way to accomplish both of these is to spend the majority of your time in the cockpit area. The common space is the default area for members of the entourage when not in their bunks, and as mentioned, the lounge in the rear is one we like to reserve for the VIP.

Bus drivers are usually pretty proficient in regards to the routes and height clearances, but keep in mind that any type of problem that occurs with the operation of the bus means that your protectee is sitting on the "X." Therefore, it is important to go over the routes with your driver in advance, paying particular attention to distances and travel times. Quite often, tour buses are used for interstate travel covering long distances, which is the primary reason for having the bunks. For those long hauls, it is typically fine for you to get some sleep as well, as in all likelihood you will be working once you reach your destination. With that said, the driver should be given strict instructions to wake you prior to any stops or deviation from the original planned route.

With some entertainers, you will be faced with the unique challenge of traveling on a wrapped bus. These are buses designed to promote an artist on tour, with promotional materials such as the artist's name and photo literally wrapped around the entirety of the bus. As you can imagine, a wrapped bus broadcasts your movements to anyone and everyone who sees it. Whenever possible, try and avoid having the protectee travel on wrapped buses.

If you have multiple buses on the tour, the case can be made to wrap one of the others, as it serves the same purpose. The one good thing about a wrapped bus is that you can use it as an effective decoy. For instance, you could stage the highly visible, wrapped bus outside of one hotel; all the fans will gravitate there assuming that the star is inside, while in fact you have your protectee securely tucked away in another hotel, having arrived there in a more nondescript bus. In essence, it's a creative way to deal with the reality of promotion without sacrificing security.

Chapter 8

POSITIONING AND WALKING WITH CLIENTS

Protectors need to understand how we exist in relationship to the principal in terms of time and space. However, before we can do that, we need to work on ourselves, so that we can rapidly and effectively respond to a threat. Psychologically, males will naturally size up other males when seeing them, just like gunslingers of the old west. The initial thought may go something like, "Could I take him if I needed to?" or "Is he stronger, smarter or faster than me?" From our perspective, we need to project an image that says, this person is a capable and switched-on protector. We also need to institute some "cheats" to give ourselves an advantage if we have to deal with an attacker or quickly move the protectee. Recall that the bad guys always have the advantage, as they get to choose the time and the place, and action has the edge over reaction.

The first thing to think about is body language and what signals we send out to others. If your hands are in your pockets or busy holding a drink, that tells one story; if your arms are folded up at chest level, that tells a different one. Now think about the story that you want to tell when you're on a protection assignment. With body language alone, you can send a nonverbal signal to a potential antagonist to help them decide to not pick you and/or your protectee to mess with. This can be achieved many times simply by how you look, how you're dressed, your body language, and your mannerisms. In short, it's possible to defeat the attack just by being you.

> The supreme art of war is to subdue the enemy without fighting. . . . Be extremely subtle even to the point of formlessness. Be extremely mysterious even to the point of soundlessness. Thereby you can be the director of the opponent's fate. . . . To win one hundred victories

in one hundred battles is not the acme of skill. To subdue the enemy without fighting is the acme of skill.

—Sun Tzu, *The Art of War*

BODY MECHANICS

As protectors, we spend the lion's share of our day walking and standing, and believe it or not, there's also a way to cheat at those. In this case, I mean being in the optimal position to respond to a threat. For the protector, a natural stance consists of legs shoulder-length apart, knees slightly bent. The idea is to look relaxed but be ready to spring into action at a moment's notice if needed. For those who have been in the military and remember standing on post, you know how taxing long hours of standing and walking can be on your feet and back. Having the knees slightly bent allows you to take some of that pressure off of your joints and spine.

The next thing you want to be mindful of is to keep your head up. A lot of people have developed what I call Smartphone Head. It's a symptom that's probably going to turn into an evolutionary condition in a few hundred years. That's when the agent's head is tilted down all the time looking at their phone. Protectors must be mindful of this and take active steps to disengage from the gravitational pull of their device.

I've also observed that some of the more physically imposing individuals in our profession tend to "shrink" a bit in public settings in an effort to make themselves less imposing. Part of that is to reduce the anxiety of people around them because of their stature, so the attempt is made to lower their profile by pulling inward. However, when working, we should strive to do the opposite. Open up, look up, get big, and be in the moment. The only time the opposite of this is true is when you are intentionally trying to lower your profile while on an assignment. However, it is the intent that drives the action, not the other way around.

If you are a protector, I should be able to look at you and say, "This guy is switched on and whoever he's with, I don't want to bother;" or, as a decision-maker, I may be thinking, "I'd like a guy like that on my team." There are times where you can land a job assignment simply because of how you look and the mannerisms you convey. The inverse is also true: you can get ruled out of opportunities because of what your body language says about your readiness, so be mindful of which image you mean to portray.

MOVING THE CLIENT

As stated before, the protective agent is responsible for the security, safety, health, and well-being of the client. Planning, preparation, and anticipation are the keys to successfully minimize risk to the principal. It is not a job of confrontation, but rather a planned response to an unavoidable situation. The object is to deter an attack or avoid a confrontation rather than expose the protectee to danger. The goal in close personal protection is to remove one's client from harm's way as quickly as possible.

Close personal protection (CPP) is a general description for professionals providing a safe, secure environment to an individual likely to encounter those who would inflict intentional or accidental harm. Close protection covers many areas, from establishing an area of security and perimeter defense, to moving formations that shield the protectee with the bodies of the men and women dedicated to ensure their safety. The best way to meet these goals is to form circles or multilayers of security around the VIP. The objective is to create a defense that will prevent a person from gaining a position wherein they are able to injure or kill the person being protected.

There are several different schools of thought into the make-up of a protective formation. With that said, the underlining principles are the same; the bodyguard is responsible for 360 degrees of body coverage in regards to the protectee. In a static environment, the optimal position for a protector is to the protectee's rear, staggered a bit to either the left or the right of the client, giving us a view of what's ahead and allowing us to shield from behind. We will want to be an arm's length away from the protectee, close enough so you can reach out and touch him or her if you need to move or shield them in a crisis situation, but not so close that if the client suddenly stops we are practically sharing the same pair of pants.

So, while that is the optimal placement when stationary, note that your position changes fluidly as you move, depending on the environment. Think of an invisible circle around the client, with you as the protector rotating into different areas within that orbit as the situation dictates.

From our starting position behind and slightly staggered, we are ready to respond in any direction. If an attack comes from the front, we will notice it, and either push forward to engage the threat or, since we're within an arm's length, cover and evacuate the protectee. If an attack comes from the rear, we will encounter it before the protectee does, again responding accordingly. Keep in mind that active scanning of a 360-degree radius requires us to intentionally look behind us.

Note that in most situations, the protectee sets the pace unless you need to rapidly move them to safety. The VIP will dictate the tempo of the movement, walking slower, or faster, or even stopping unexpectedly or abruptly. As you move, take care to not step on your client's heels; instead, try to anticipate their stride so that you are matching it. Conversely, make it a point not to lag too far behind the client so that you would have to sprint to catch up if you need to respond quickly to a situation. The reality is, there are some VIPs who will find your constant presence a bit of an irritant, particularly in the beginning, but if you are doing the job properly, they will soon forget that you are even there.

As noted, the protectee normally dictates the tempo, and as a behavioral trait, these individuals don't want to be led; instead, they are instinctive pack leaders. The challenge is that, in many cases, they don't know where they are supposed to be going. So how do you deal with the fact that they don't want to be led, but don't have a clue about how they are getting there?

One suggestion is that you will want to refrain from tapping or otherwise touching them to indicate the proper direction. When you consider all the movements that you do in a typical day, all that touching is going to get annoying to the protectee rather quickly. Additionally, in some cultures, physical touch is taboo, particularly when protecting the opposite sex. We still need to convey the direction we want the client to go in, though, and I have found that the best way when operating from a position behind them is to extend a hand into their field of view and gesture slightly in the direction you want them to move. Similar to a car's navigation system, the protectee has their attention focused elsewhere, but in their peripheral vision, they see the changes that you're indicating.

This way, the client gets to feel like he has his independence, but still does not end up walking into walls or, worse yet, exiting the wrong door and walking right into a horde of screaming fans. I have clients who never look up, because they are always in their iPhone or reading a script or contract, yet they always get to where they are going, because I've given them a human GPS by way of subtle hand gestures.

Sometimes a brief word or two, "This way, sir," will help, but again think of it like the prompt on a vehicle navigation, a small chirp and that's it. I suggest refraining from chatting constantly with the VIP. One reason is that if you're always talking, they can get used to the sound of your voice and subsequently may not pay full attention to you when it is absolutely necessary. If you keep your communications to a minimum, when you do speak, they will tune in. Use a low monotone; with little change of facial expression. Remember the adage (which I've modified slightly): speak and walk softly, and carry a big stick.

There are occasionally times when you're on a movement and you will need to touch the client, say, to prevent them from tripping over an obstruction such as a cable or walking into a cobblestone street in heels. If this is required, I recommend using two fingers, giving them a little bit of pressure in the small of their back just to put them back on the correct course. When used subtly and in a reserved manner, the client will appreciate that you respect his or her space, and then continue to go about his or her day. If there is snow or ice on the walking path, it is sound advice to keep a hand near the VIP's back (about half an inch away) to lend them balance and support should they slip. In certain circumstances, it may be necessary and permissible to assist the client by taking his or her hand, forearm, or elbow to support him or her.

With additional personnel, our optimal placement remains the same, as this position gives us the best vantage point for carrying out our mandate of covering and evacuating the protectee if everything goes to hell.

One might think that if you have two agents on the team, and there is a threat, that both agents collapse on the protectee to provide body cover. However, what that does is leave the threat unmitigated, and the attack could proceed as planned. Imagine an assailant with a firearm; if both security people move to cover the protectee, it's literally like shooting crabs in a barrel.

You can most often see an example of this in night clubs. If there is a fight at the club, all the bouncers immediately rush to the area where the altercation is. What that does by default is leave the other areas unprotected, and that's when somebody opens the back door and lets people in, robs the cash box, or a host of other mishaps. This was due to the fact that everybody in security at that club was trained to do the exact same role. If something happens, they all go to deal with it, leaving these big gaps in coverage.

While there are several schools of thought, my philosophy is that, even when working in smaller teams with celebrities and high net-worth individuals, there is only one bodyguard on the team. Think about it like football; there is only one quarterback for the team on the field at one time. The bodyguard is responsible for the protectee, with 360-degree coverage, additional members of the close protection team are called security escorts or simply escorts. An escort is for all intents and purposes an extra set of eyes, ears, and hands for the bodyguard. The escort is the one who, when we walk to a door, makes sure that the door isn't locked, or when we get ready to hit a corner, is the first to encounter that blind spot, and so forth.

The security escort is positioned in front of the client, staggered either to the left or to the right, optimally on the opposite side of where the bodyguard is, so that the bodyguard can have a clearer line of sight. Accordingly, he's also not standing directly in front of the protectee, because then the client would spend the majority of his day staring at the back of the security escort's head.

The escort's area of responsibility is directly ahead and 90 degrees to the left and to the right. With that said, he does have to worry about the protectee going off course, because even with him leading, as mentioned above, the protectee still dictates the tempo. Another instance where developing your peripheral vision is going to come in handy.

While the front escort has 180 degrees of responsibility, that does not mean that the bodyguard is now just responsible for the rear half of the circle. In fact, the bodyguard is still wholly responsible for 360 degrees of coverage and cannot absolve themselves of that responsibility. The escort is just additional help.

If you are in the security escort role and the client deviates from the direction of travel so that you find yourself out of position, simply open up your stride and veer back on course, reassuming your position. Since this most certainly will happen, just make the adjustment; outside of an emergency, there's no need to run to get back into that front escort position. Running could make the protectee nervous, and if you start running, they may think that they need to start running as well, and you could see how that could turn into an issue.

While on a movement, we need to again make sure of our nonverbal cues, this time with passersby. As we are moving, we should also be actively observing everyone in close proximity, and resist the urge to drop our gaze as we pass people (a societal courtesy). My philosophy is that I want them to know that I am looking at them. In fact, just them keying in on the protector in the act of active observation can dissuade the person from doing something you don't want them to do.

As protectors, we need to mentally acknowledge all nonvetted individuals in our client's personal space as potential threats, but one thing we don't want to do is to attract unnecessary attention. As such, resist the urge to speak to people as you are passing them. That stereotype in the movies where a burly bodyguard whisks his client through a room, saying, "Move out of the way," (even if it would be easier for him to direct his client around the obstacle) can often bring undue attention when none was called for.

Vocalizing may actually cause passersby to recognize your client when they otherwise had no idea who was moving though the area. There will be times when you do need to issue some verbal commands, but that is to dissuade, not invite, and oftentimes, just a look will be enough.

If you find the need to speak, choose your words deliberately; you would be surprised how utterances like "please," "thank you," and "pardon me" open up doors and diffuse potentially volatile situations. As such, the other party has an increased likelihood to be more compliant, and this also reduces resentment against your client (aka, "who does this person think they are?) Manners are more than courtesy; they are a strategic solution to a situation.

Don't be of one of those who think their client is the most important person in the world, and therefore believes that makes him or her the second most important person in the world. This mentality leads to the individual drawing attention to himself by talking loudly or behaving in a manner that attracts onlookers, in essence forgetting that they should be moving as a shadow. In their mind, being seen with a highly recognized person elevates their own stature, and they relish the potential publicity, rarely thinking of the negative consequences these actions create.

"He who wishes to fight must first count the cost."
—Sun Tzu, The Art of War

PREVENTING PROBLEMS BEFORE THEY HAPPEN

Imagine a soccer game; for those familiar with the sport, you know that when it's game time, most of the action takes place in the middle of the field. While the back and forth is going on, alternating between offense and defense, the two goalies are at the opposing ends of the field, waiting. Even so, during the times that the action isn't in his immediate vicinity, you won't find the goalie checking his phone, grabbing a seat on the turf, or slipping his phone number to a female fan. Instead, before the ball comes anywhere near him, the goalie is scanning and analyzing. He's planning eventualities and probabilities, so that if different situations come up, he'll know what to do in response. In essence, he's playing the "what if" game, analyzing the situation and constantly making adjustments as needed so that when the ball does come, he's ready to intercept it.

To me, this is the perfect analogy for protection work. Most of the time, nothing monumental is happening; however, when that moment of truth comes, you have to respond quickly and effectively. You have to keep your head in the game even when it seems like everything is routine. The time is always now, meaning that you need to be fully in the moment, awake, and alert, because if an unfavorable situation presents itself, you need to act. Not a second too early, not a second too late, but existing in the now.

Despite all the preparation in the world, there are times when you will be up against a determined adversary, whether that's an obsessive fan or someone bent on violence to your protectee. That's when you will need to take decisive action.

REACTING TO THREATS

So, what happens when that *potential* threat (an unvetted individual in your VIP's space) turns into a confirmed threat and we have to very quickly get the protectee the hell out of the area? Remember, unlike most other "Alpha" professions, our job is not to confront, but instead get the client out of harm's way as rapidly as possible. Of course, the situation and the environment might determine that we have to stay and fight, but successful flight in this instance would be considered a mission success. So, if we are moving with the protectee and a threat emerges, we will need to shield the VIP while simultaneously conducting a hard movement or turn, commonly referred to as Cover and Evacuation.

From whichever direction the attack comes from, the protector will want to provide body cover and move the VIP away from the threat. Within our optimal position of arm's length away, the first thing you want to do is to close the gap, meaning eliminate the space between your body and the clients. Once you've done that, next establish positive control of the protectee by getting a firm grip on him or her, and do not worry about being polite. If there is an immediate threat, deal with the situation, and you can apologize for the rough handling later.

Keep in mind that the protectee might clinch up and go into freeze mode, essentially rooting themselves in place. To counter that, you will want to take them off balance by using their body mechanics to your advantage. To do that, lower their center of gravity by bending them slightly forward at the waist, being careful not to fold them over completely. Bend them too much and if you need to start moving, they might nosedive right into the concrete.

If you are reacting to a hostile threat that requires you to do the above, now is not the time to be quiet. Instead, you need to tell the protectee what you want them to do in forceful, direct, and easy-to-understand language. In this case: "MOVE," and while issuing that imperative, rapidly take the protectee in the direction you want while maintaining positive control.

As you are moving the protectee, you will also need to shield them with your body, and while your human instinct tells you to protect yourself from getting shot, stabbed, or otherwise injured, this is the moment of truth for you as a protector. Depending on the situation, how you rise to this occasion could literally be the difference between life and death. In terms of body coverage, one simple rule is to attempt to get big while making the protectee get small. Yet again, another case to be made for the protector who wears body armor regularly.

ATTACKS ON PRINCIPAL (AOP)

> I feel so cold and I long for your embrace; I keep crying, "Baby, baby, please" Oh, can't you see you belong to me; How my poor heart aches with every step you take; Every move you make and every vow you break; Every smile you fake, every claim you stake, I'll be watching you.
> —*Every Breath You Take* (The Police, Synchronicity, 1983)

Stalking

From the outside looking in, the celebrity client has everything he or she might want: talent, good looks, fame and fortune. However, all of that is wonderful until they attract the unwanted attention of the obsessive individual whose illusions drive them to attempt to make contact in an uncomfortable and, in some cases, deadly encounter. The roles become the hunted (sometimes knowingly, oftentimes not), and the hunter, in pursuit of the object of his fantasy fulfillment.

Domestic and celebrity stalking is defined as pursuing by stalking; to pursue obsessively and to the point of harassment.[1] Stalking is criminal activity consisting of the repeated following and harassing of another person. It is a distinctive form activity composed of a series of actions that, taken individually, might constitute legal behavior; for example, sending flowers, writing love notes, and waiting for someone outside her place of work are all actions that, on their own, are not criminal. When these actions are coupled with an intent to instill fear or injury, however, they may constitute a pattern of behavior that is illegal. Though anti-stalking laws are gender neutral, most stalkers are men and most victims are women.[2]

Stalking refers to the activity in which someone is repeatedly followed, harassed, or physically threatened by another person. The stalker may be a stranger with a romantic fixation on the victim or an ex-lover or estranged spouse who does not want to end the relationship.[3]

---

1. Retrieved 03/12/18 from https://www.merriam-webster.com/dictionary/stalking
2. Retrieved 03/14/18 from http://legal-dictionary.thefreedictionary.com/Stalking-
3. Gilligan, Matthew J. (1992). Stalking the Stalkers. *Georgia Law Review, 27.* Quoted in Fuller, John Randolph (2008). *Criminal Justice; Mainstream and Crosscurrents; Annotated Instructor's Edition.* Upper Saddle River NJ: Pearson-Prentice Hall.

Dr. Park E. Dietz, a forensic psychiatrist and a respected authority on mass murderers and stalkers, has defined three specific subtypes of the romantic stalker that can be practically applied in an attempt to better understand the motivations of such a criminal:

1. The spurned ex-lover or spouse, whose primary motivation is revenge against the person who has rejected or offended him or her.
2. The individual who is suffering from a delusional disorder, who will engage in bizarre and clearly unrealistic fantasies, often believing he or she is involved in a love relationship with a prominent or symbolic individual.
3. The individual suffering from a pathological dependence on another, who becomes obsessed with the target of his or her dependence and finds it difficult or impossible to function without the attention and companionship of that person.[4]

Some of the more commonly reported stalking behaviors include:

- Unwanted approach at home, school, the workplace, etc.
- Unwanted telephone calls, including hang-up
- Unwanted text or voice messages
- Watching or following the victim from a distance
- Spying on the victim with a listening device, camera, or global positioning system (GPS)
- Unwanted emails, instant messages, or messaging through social media websites
- Leaving strange or threatening items for the victim to find
- Sending or leaving unwanted cards, letters, flowers, or presents
- Trespassing or breaking into the victim's car or home and then doing something that would alert the victim to the intrusion[5]

---

4. Retrieved 03/14/18 from workplaceviolence911.com/sites/workplaceviolence911.com/files/20010406-19_1.htm

5. Dana, Steven, J. Protection From Abuse Security Services; Domestic Violence & Stalking–A Potentially Deadly Combination; March 2017. Retrieved 5/29/17 from https://protection-fromabuse.org/blog/uncategorized/domestic-violence-stalking-part-ii-a-potentially-deadly-combination/

Psychological Mindfulness of Stalkers

Paul Mullen, clinical director and chief psychiatrist at Australia's Victoria's Forensicare, a high-security hospital for mentally ill offenders, has studied stalkers and established five recognizable sub-categories.[6]

1. Rejected stalking type as an individual who has experienced the unwanted end of a close relationship, most likely with a romantic partner, but also with a parent, work associate, or acquaintance. When this stalker's attempts to reconcile fail, they frequently seek revenge.
2. Intimacy seeker identifies a person, often a complete stranger, as their true love and begins to behave as if they are in a relationship with that person. Many intimacy-seeking stalkers carry the delusion that their love is reciprocated.
3. Incompetent subtype, like the intimacy seeker, hopes their behavior would lead to a close relationship, satisfying their need for contact and intimacy. However, this type of stalker acknowledges that their victim is not reciprocating their affection while they still continue their pursuit. Mullen views these stalkers as intellectually limited and socially awkward. Given their inability to comprehend and carry out socially normal and accepted courting rituals, the incompetent stalker uses methods that are often counterproductive and frightening.
4. Resentful stalker experiences feelings of injustice and desires revenge against their victim rather than a relationship. Their behavior reflects their perception that they have been humiliated and treated unfairly, viewing themselves as the victim.
5. Predator stalker also has no desire for a relationship with their victims, but a sense of power and control. Mullen explains that they find pleasure in gathering information about their victim and fantasizing about assaulting them physically, and most frequently sexually.

---

6. Muller, Robert T. Ph.D. (2013). In the Mind of a Stalker; Revealing the five types of stalkers. Article retrieved 5/29/17 from psychologytoday.com/blog/talking-about-trauma/201306/in-the-mind-stalker

Erotomania is a delusion in which one person believes another (usually of a higher social status or a celebrity) is in love with them. The targeted person may not even know that the stalker exists. Clinically speaking, the stalker may be schizophrenic or suffer other psychotic delusional disorders including bipolar tendencies.

John Hinckley is an example of the incompetent subtype. Hinckley stalked actress Jody Foster but was rebuffed in all his efforts to draw her attention. He believed that if he did something spectacular and gained publicity, Foster would come to know him and return his love. On March 30, 1981 Hinckley attempted to assassinate President Reagan and was later determined to be legally insane, resulting in incarceration and treatment at St. Elizabeth's Hospital in Washington, D.C. until 2017.

There is another type of stalker: the kind who will follow his intended victim for the purpose of assassination; a political assassin or a professional "hit man." Arthur Bremer is an example of an amateur stalker and potential assassin. From his diary, it was found that he stalked President Nixon to several cities with the intent of shooting the president. On one occasion, Bremer went into a restroom before he would attempt to get close enough to the president to carry out his endeavor. In the restroom, he saw a man dressed in a suit, whom Bremer assumed was a Secret Service agent. That was sufficient to deter him from his attack. On another occasion, in Ottawa, Canada, Bremer was diverted when he concluded security was too tight. After that, he changed his target focus. In Silver Spring, Maryland he shot and paralyzed Governor George Wallace, who was campaigning for the presidential nomination.

An interesting point for consideration is that a professional assassin or hit man will plan his attack to include a provision for escape, whereas an amateur, like Bremer, or a celebrity stalker, plans up to the event or timing of confrontation but doesn't plan for the consequences of being caught or intercepted.

A majority of stalking campaigns begin very subtly, and victims feel nothing more than annoyance. When they finally realize what is happening, they become intimidated and they can't help but feel helpless and frustrated.

Celebrity Stalking

Celebrity stalking is a symptom of our image-dominated culture. There are numerous websites devoted to it, and some participants think that celebrities deserve it, and they are emboldened in their commentary due to the anonymity of social media. As fans accept the thinning of personal boundaries via blogs, social pages, and intrusive videos, there develops a parallel increase in their desire to trespass into the lives of the rich and famous. . . . As the loss of privacy in our culture converges with the demand to know every detail about celebrity lives, we can expect to see more stalkers, some of whom will certainly be lethal.[7]

Similarly, we read:

Living in the limelight exposes celebrities to the prying eyes and make them easy victims for stalkers. Moreover, the advancement in technology has led to a rise in stalking, especially thanks to social networks and cell phones.

The entertainment industry has a record of instances of stalking by obsessive individuals who have harassed, threatened, and even stabbed and shot the objects of their displaced admiration and love. The following cases of celebrity stalking are so frightening and bizarre that we must strongly sympathize with the traumatized celebrities.[8]

Madonna

Robert Dewey Hoskins stalked Madonna in the '90s and threatened to slit her throat, but her security team shot him in the leg after he jumped the fence.

Justin Bieber

In 2010, prison inmate Dana Martin, who served a sentence for the brutal rape and murder of a 15-year-old girl, became obsessed with Justin Bieber. After several unsuccessful attempts to connect with the singer, Martin decided he wanted the pop star dead. He conspired

---

7. Ramsland, Katherine. Celebrity Stalkers. *Psychology Today;* February 11, 2011; Retrieved 9/23/17 from psychologytoday.com/blog/shadow-boxing/201202/celebrity-stalkers
8. Retrieved 12/28/17 from hallofgossip.com/celebrities-who-have-been-stalked

with another inmate, Mark Staake, and Mark's nephew, Tanner Ruane, to find Mr. Bieber, execute him, and cut off his genitals as a trophy. Martin, Staake, and Ruane were all charged with multiple counts of first-degree conspiracy to commit murder.

Catherine Zeta-Jones and Michael Douglas

They dealt with a crazed stalker named Dawnette Knight, who became obsessed with Douglas and believed that Zeta-Jones only married him for his money. Knight sent some disturbing letters to the actress, detailing how she would cut her up into pieces and feed her to dogs if she didn't leave Douglas. Knight was sentenced to three years in prison.

Gwyneth Paltrow

For nearly two decades, Dante Soiu stalked Gwyneth Paltrow. He sent the actress threatening letters saying he wanted to use "God's scalpel to cut sin out of her" and sent sex toys and other lewd gifts to her home. He even showed up at her mother's house.

Taylor Swift

Taylor Swift received a restraining order against a man who believed he was married to Taylor and vowed to murder anyone who came between them. He sent her emails, letters, and tweets saying frightening things like: "If anyone in Taylor Swift's family gets killed, it is not my fault," and "My wife, Taylor Swift (Sweet) and I live in Beverly Hills. I am in love with her. In conclusion, we treat each other with dignity and respect. I will carry a gun to protect her the rest of my life."

WHY DO PEOPLE WORSHIP CELEBRITIES?

People often look for ways to escape the stressors in their lives and, in this way, celebrities are able to tap into the basic emotions of people and give them a reprieve from their everyday trials. By engaging with them through media, the worshipper is able to live in a sort of fantasy world entertaining hidden wishes and aspirations.

Another reason people may turn to celebrity worship is their own sense of isolation. As society becomes less connected emotionally, people may be filling communal needs by becoming attached to celebrities and larger-than-life personalities. After all, many people feel like they have grown up with certain characters on television or artists through their professional careers.

In short, many people experience harmless celebrity worship by following their favorite movie or pop star on their journey though the entertainment industry. The problem comes when people feel so isolated and alone that they must connect with somebody who is, for all intents and purposes, out of reach. As a result, many professionals contend that the foundations of celebrity worship are rooted in our culture's social inadequacies.

THREE LEVELS OF CELEBRITY WORSHIP

Evidence indicates that poor mental health is associated with unhealthy levels of celebrity worship. The types or levels of celebrity worship are as follows:

Entertainment-Social

This level of celebrity worship is relatively harmless and involves reading or learning about celebrities, talking with friends about celebrities, or becoming part of a celebrity fan club.

Intense-Personal

This level reflects a deepening illusion surrounding a celebrity. Often the worshipper will believe that they have a special bond with the celebrity, and when they see something bad happen to the celebrity in the media, they may feel like it is happening to them as well.

Borderline-Pathological

This level of worship is typified by obsessive thoughts about a celebrity that the worshipper cannot stop even though they may try. These thoughts often lead to delusional beliefs. Often the worshipper expects the celebrity to come to their home or believes that the celebrity is in love with them. Stalking behavior is commonly associated when a person reaches borderline-pathological level."[9]

FANS VERSUS OBSESSIVE FANS

In this day and time, the entertainment business is a two-way relationship built between the entertainer and their fans, with the protector standing as a buffer between the two. In a perfect world, there would be no need for protectors when entertainers are dealing with the adoring public. We could just focus our attention on those intentionally trying to do the protectee harm. But, in reality, we have to also keep a close eye on those who would describe themselves as fans as well. Even the word "fan" is loaded, originally derived from the word "fanatic," which originally meant, inspired by God and also, furiously mad. So, while it is a given that celebrities will have admirers, we have to distinguish between what is normal and what is obsessive.

We also have to keep the big picture in mind when we think about fans, and remember who pays the bills. A strong fan base of a popular client, particularly if they are younger and animated, can give protectors an endless series of headaches. Therefore, the challenge is to figure how not to develop an antagonistic relationship with them, where you start to detest the ones who ultimately pay your client's bills, and therefore yours.

It goes without saying that the obsessive fans are the ones to look out for and pay close attention to. They fixate on celebrities and public figures, acting out in ways that could cause unintentional or, on the extreme side, intentional harm.

Part of the problem stems from the demand on the business side of the entertainment industry. As mentioned earlier, music and movies aren't selling the way they did in the past, so the management teams, record companies, and the film agencies strongly encourage the artists under their rosters to interact more with their fans. These days, the lion's share of that interaction happens through social media, but it's also there where the message can get lost in translation and distorted. When the artist says, "I love you" on Twitter, most people just under-

---

9. Murphy, Melissa. The Psychology Behind Celebrity Worship. Retrieved 05/29/17 from https://celebrities.knoji.com/the-psychology-behind-celebrity-worship/

stand that they mean it in a general sense. To the obsessive fan, however, when that star says, "I love you," they think they're talking specifically to them.

For the modern protector, it's not enough to learn how to shoot semi-automatic rifles and do fancy dropkicks. Now, more than ever before, we have to roll up our sleeves and dig deep into what is called protective intelligence. That means also having a working understanding of new media, specifically social media. We need to know the difference between Twitter and Instagram and Snapchat. Even if you may not use them personally, you still need to be aware of them and how they work, because that's the method of communication that fans, both normal and obsessive, are using.

A savvy fan using social media can find out when a VIP is in a certain area just by monitoring the celebrity's tweets, and the more obsessive ones can interpret that as an invitation. The platform itself plays into that engagement as well; when a celebrity says, "I love you," to all his fans, that obsessive fan can respond immediately back to the VIP's verified account with, "I love you, too!" The celebrity never notices this, because they're getting thousands of messages from fans all over the world and can't possibly read them all. So, to the celebrity, it's a one-way broadcast, but to that obsessive fan, who's received a message beamed directly to her personal device, it's more like, "OMG! He's talking right to me, and I'm talking right to him!"

That's where the problem lies. So, when the celebrity says, "Catch me at midnight at this great party in North Hollywood," this type of fan thinks the invite is uniquely and specifically for them. They get dressed up and go to the event, along with thousands of others, and after paying the hefty admission fee, they are disappointed to find that the VIP is sequestered in a section behind the DJ booth with restricted access. The obsessive fan now feels deflated, embarrassed, and betrayed—and this could be a recipe for problems down the road.

Another concern is location-based social media. The godfather of this was an application called Four Square, which originally started out as a run-of-the-mill geo-tagging service. Geo-tagging is the process of obtaining geographical/location data and adding it to various media. Four Square turned this technology into a game of sorts: you went to a place, you "checked in," and you said to the world, "Hey, I'm here." In return, you might get an award or prize; for instance, a free doughnut if you checked in at the same restaurant five times in a week, or a virtual badge of honor if you frequented a certain coffee spot. The challenge is that anyone who "followed" you could see exactly where you were and the places you frequent. That sharing of location-based data in the wrong hands can lead to serious security concerns.

Facebook has now joined the geo-tagging business with its "Check In" feature, and Instagram, the popular photo sharing site, makes it easy for users to geo-tag their location and attach their whereabouts to uploaded photos. Using these apps, the unthinking celebrity client checks in, essentially telling the world exactly where they are at a given moment. From a security point of view, it presents a quantifiable risk. We as protectors have to understand how these services work; if not, we won't be able to advise our clients or monitor the chatter and conversations taking place as they relate to the protectee.

There was a serious incident a few years ago with the tech giant Oracle, a corporation that spends millions of dollars annually protecting their CEO. On this occasion, the 41st richest man in the world was likely surprised to learn that his teenage children had been posting photos of their wonderful life, including their home and trips, to their social media accounts—with the geo-tagging on. This told people two things: (1) where they were at any given moment, and (2) where they weren't. A motivated perpetrator could hit the residence, knowing that the home was empty. The post also increased the risk of kidnapping, because it told anyone interested exactly where the children were.

CHRISTINA GRIMMIE KILLED BY OBSESSED STALKER, KEVIN LOIBL

Christina Victoria Grimmie, an American singer, songwriter, musician, actress, and YouTuber known for her participation in the NBC singing competition, *The Voice*, was fatally shot and killed in Orlando, Florida on June 10, 2016 by her stalker, Kevin Loibl.

Loibl thought he and Grimmie were meant to be together, and a friend often heard him make the suggestion. He was said to have grown increasingly more obsessed with Grimmie over the last year, watching any and all videos of her. The killer never elaborated on what he would do if he met Christina, but he referred to her as his "soul mate."[10]

The friend also said that Loibl once told him that if there was a God, he "has seen it in [Grimmie]." Loibl went to great lengths to be physically appealing to Grimmie. According to TMZ, the killer underwent hair transplants, got Lasik eye surgery, adopted a vegan diet to lose weight, and often discussed with co-workers marrying the star. He listened to her music during his shifts and claimed he had contact with her through an online video game.[11]

"I CAN MAKE YOU LOVE ME"–
THE STORY OF LAURA BLACK

Laura Black, a recent college graduate with dreams and aspirations, was an attractive employee of Electromagnetic Systems Labs (ESL) in Sunnyvale, California. A co-employee, Richard Farley, according to him, "fell in love with her at first sight . . . it was her smile." For two years, Farley pursued and stalked Laura, who rebuffed his efforts to date her. He sent her gifts and flowers, followed her, even attending her cardio class. His activities were reported to the corporate human resources department, and he was eventually fired, and a restraining order against him was issued. At the time, there were no laws against stalking and, as a result, the restraining order was Laura's only recourse.

The order infuriated him more than the firing, and he swore to take vengeance against Laura and her employer, stating that a restraining order was "merely a piece of paper and would not stop bullets." Farley sold his truck and bought weapons, including a shotgun, a high-powered rifle, two semi-automatic pistols, and ammunition.

A local newspaper summarized the ordeal of Laura and ESL on that fatal day of February 16, 1988.[12]

---

10. Retrieved 06/24/18/ from https://www.quora.com/What-is-the-reason-behind-the-killing-of-The-Voices-Christina-Grimmie-1
11. Retrieved 06/24/18/ from https://www.quora.com/What-is-the-reason-behind-the-killing-of-The-Voices-Christina-Grimmie-1
12. Retrieved 05//27/17. For more information regarding the full story, see http://www.workplaceviolence911.com/sites/workplaceviolence911.com/files/20010406-19_1.htm

February 17, 1988, SUNNYVALE, Calif.—A man's obsession for a woman who spurned his love ignited a violent spasm of gunfire that left seven people dead and four others wounded at a high-security military plant here Tuesday, police investigators said today.

"He said he was in love with her from the first moment he saw her— it was her smile," said Lieut. Ruben Grijalva, a Sunnyvale Public Safety Department hostage negotiator. Lieutenant Grijalva said he persuaded the man, Richard W. Farley, to surrender almost six hours after he took over a sprawling two-story building at the ESL Inc. plant here in a hail of gunfire.

"He knew she was not attracted to him," Lieutenant Grijalva added, "but he told her it wouldn't end until either she went out with him or he died."[13]

The Farley-Black stalking case eventually resulted in the governor of California signing the first anti-stalking law.

PROTECTIVE INTELLIGENCE AND ASSESSMENT

It has easily been established that the better known and celebrated a person becomes, the greater the potential risks and vulnerability to his or her life and safety. Protective intelligence is the first step in nullifying threatening encounters. Intelligence consists of data and information that has been gathered and analyzed, producing well thought-out conclusions and recommendations. The data can consist of facts complied from a variety of open and specialty sources such as snippets of news and social media postings, police departmental reports and sharing, as well as any direct communications (telephone calls, email, letters) sent to the celebrity.

Intelligence gathering should be initiated when a protective detail begins as part of the overall protective umbrella. The first interview with the celebrity and her staff will define any preexisting concerns and threats including recently fired employees, known disgruntled fans, and any suspicious packages, letters, and emails previously received. All this information will, when analyzed, help build a profile

---

13. Retrieved 5/27/17 from murderpedia.org/male.F/f/farley-richard.htm

that can be cross-referenced with any new potential concerns and people of interest.

With elevated concerns, the need may require reaching out to larger police departments that have a protective intelligence division responsible for collecting and correlating threats made to VIPs and celebrities. Depending on the escalations, there may be a need to notify federal agencies such as the FBI in hopes that their resources may provide information leading to the identity of the threat.

When a threat is made and the identity of the perpetrator is known, should the person making the threat be interviewed? This is an interesting question because of the potential consequences. Will the interview and presence of the protector increase or deflect the threat? Will the instigator become more hostile and determined, or will he heed the intent of the interview? The same questions arise about the service of a restraining order. These are serious considerations and must be given adequate thought to all potential consequences.

In the instance of the Laura Black-Richard Farley stalking and attack cited earlier, Farley was interviewed by Human Resources and served with a restraining order, both of which were not only ineffective but they also raised his level of determination for vengeance.

The advantage of a personal interview, especially in the event of a letter writer, is that the perception of the writer may change. In his letters he may be bold, threatening, and seemingly dangerous; however, in person he may be timid and fearful, physically unable to carry out any of his insults and threats. The same questions arise about a stalker; an interview about his intents and purpose may dissuade him from further stalking activity, or it could push him into a more covert method. Choose your method of intervention wisely.

Chapter 9

RED CARPET EVENTS

There is a whole set of protocols, both written and implied, for red carpet events. If you know these rules, you can save yourself and your client both time and frustration. If you don't, you'll find yourself literally on the outside looking in until the event is over.

Here's a little-known fact: most major award shows these days don't allow the celebrities' personal security on the red carpet. The reason is that many protectors don't know how to navigate and interact on the red carpet and end up becoming the clog in a well-oiled machine. Therefore, the event planners have had to deal with it in their own way, with the current model having the VIP's security team hand the protectee off to the event staff, essentially absolving us of our responsibilities. The problem with this is that we have no idea what level of training the people we are handing our clients over to have. Do not get me wrong—there are some amazingly talented professionals who work event security, but there are also barely trained staff that may have been hired a week before the event.

If you want to provide the best protection for your client, you need to understand the anatomy and protocol of the red carpet so that you can actually make it onto the carpet. This is not about bragging rights or so that you can be a part of the experience. In fact, it's the *shiny thing syndrome* that often dooms a lot of protectors in the celebrity arena, particularly when it comes to award shows.

Despite all the glitter, we can't get star-struck. You have to remind yourself that with all the fanfare going on, you are there to do a job. That's not just a challenge for new people, sometimes it can actually be harder for those of us who have been in the industry a long time, because we've done so many of these events that we can be lulled into thinking that "I've got this," and let our guard down.

Figure 9.1. Celebrity protection takes many shapes and forms, and the touring element is not to be overlooked as it's both a means of gaining experience and a great revenue generator.

Figure 9.2. Tour Buses bring a whole new dynamic to moving the protectee from point A to point B.

Figure 9.3. Demonstrating the Arm's Length Away philosophy when it comes to fan interactions on the red carpet.

Figure 9.4. An example of an award show seating chart, complete with placeholders for VIP talent.

Figure 9.5. By land, sea or Gulfstream IV, the protector's job takes many forms, and waiting is usually a part.

Figure 9.6. When the protectee interacts with the fans during a performance, we have to find ways to be close enough to react, but not so close that we interfere with the show.

Figure 9.7. The security escort surveys the receiving line, looking for that which is out of place.

Figure 9.8. The Arm's Length Away philosophy on the red carpet requires close attention to be paid to the hands and the eyes, with distance and client proximity playing a major factor.

THE RED CARPET

Before you and your client get into the actual awards show, there's the grand entrance on the carpet itself. Incidentally, the carpets are not always red; on one occasion, there was a lime green carpet—I think it was because the sponsor wanted to promote how eco-friendly it was. Whatever the color, that carpet is the way in for your client—and, with some preparation, for you.

It's the big day, and now comes the big arrival of your VIP to the carpet. The limo pulls up, your client is greeted by the publicist and a production coordinator, and they wave at you and tell you they have it from here. That's usually the story for many in the profession, which is due to the awards, historically speaking, having issues with bodyguards who don't know how to navigate the carpet with their client, and basically being more trouble than they are worth.

With that said, if you know what I term the *choreography of the carpet* and have the blessing of the client's handlers and the production department, you can gain full escort privileges, taking the client from the carpet to the entrance and, in some cases, beyond.

Red carpet arrivals are usually divided into three stages, each with its own protocols and unwritten rules: these consist of cordoned off areas or "pools" containing sections for photographers, interviewers, and fans. The order in which you encounter them may be different depending on the type of award show, and in some cases one or more elements might be omitted, but familiarizing yourself with these three will prepare you for most encounters.

PHOTOGRAPHERS

While we spend our whole career doing our best to keep clients off the "X" (where that X represents a vulnerable location), on this occasion, we have to do the exact opposite, because the "X" on the carpet isn't there to indicate danger; in fact, it literally marks the spot.

Everyone has seen the red carpet events where the handsome actor or the beautiful starlet stops, takes several photos in a variety of poses, then moves down a bit further. What you might not notice is that there is a method for how they are actually moving down the carpet.

As always, we protectors are responsible for 360 degrees of coverage. The challenge here is to maintain that coverage without being in the photographers' way. This boils down to positioning yourself out of the frame of the photos being taken. The problem most protectors have is that they are way too close to the VIP who is moving down the carpet, thus ruining the shot.

How do you know where to stand? Start with knowing where the client will be standing, and that's where that "X" comes in. All but invisible to television watchers, many times (but not always) the red carpet has little marks indicating the position where they want the talent to stand to give the photo-hogs the ideal shot. After several photos are taken, the idea is for the VIP to move to the next mark, and so on, and so on.

Traditionally, it's the publicist or the production rep who moves the talent. But if you understand how the system works, you can move your client and therefore have an actual reason (in their mind) for being on the red carpet. Think about it, on one of the biggest nights in their industry, the publicist might have anywhere from 5 to 10 other clients to also shepherd through this process. They would actually be grateful to have someone lighten their load—that is, if they were confident that you knew what you were doing. Another bonus is that, ticket or not, once you are already on the carpet itself, it's less likely that someone will tell you that you need to wait outside of the main event space.

Bear in mind that the carpet is not always visibly marked, and in those situations, you will need to do a little quick math in your head. Mentally divide the carpet into sections and split the group of photographers into roughly equal parts. Your process would then be to direct your client to the first spot—click-click-click—and then move them to the next. How long you spend is determined by a variety of factors, such as how long before the show begins, your client's position in relation to the talent in front of you, how many people are waiting behind you, and so forth. Your gut is going to be the biggest determining factor, but the ideal pacing is only going to come from the repetition of doing it.

Unfortunately, you will find out the hard way if you are too close to the protectee during this process. Imagine that the photojournalists have been waiting all night to catch your celebrity client in his Oscar outfit, and now some unknown guy (you) is in the shot. The paparazzi have learned to quickly express their displeasure that an adjustment needs to be made, by being vocal about it, namely in the form of booing.

The booing is a prompt, like honking a car horn, to pay attention and get out of the way. Unfortunately, to the general public, it can actually appear that they are booing the VIP. The next day, the society column reads, "Celebrity XYZ Booed on Red Carpet." Something like that is almost a guarantee that you will be told to wait in the car the next time . . . if there is a next time for you.

INTERVIEWS

The next stop on the carpet is the Interview section. These are usually conducted by a team of two, a journalist or other television personality holding a microphone and conducting the interview, and a cameraperson filming the conversation. Occasionally a third person, the segment producer, is present to make sure things run smoothly.

With a multitude of organizations present during an awards show, it's unlikely that your client will do all of the interviews in this section, simply due to time constraints. As such, a great rule of thumb is to learn in advance which news organizations the protectee will not be doing interviews with. This method is easier than trying to keep all of the various organizations in your head. The client might do *ABC, Entertainment Weekly,* and *USA Today,* but wish to avoid TMZ or any controversial bloggers who might try to raise sensitive or embarrassing issues that are best avoided. Let's say your client's recently released song contains lyrics that some have perceived as anti-religious. You want to steer them clear of an interview with the *Religious Times Network.*

Of course, it's not up to you to make this decision; this information should be conveyed from the manager, agent, or publicist in advance. However, just you asking the question will show the powers that be that you are not only thinking of the client's physical safety, but are also protecting the client's brand. You now have another reason to be on the carpet, as you direct the VIP to the first few interview marks and then conveniently put your body towards the camera as you whisk your client past the organizations on the "naughty" list. This way, you are the bad guy, not your client and not the publicist, who would otherwise have to bear that brunt and make excuses. Most interviewers are professionals, and they know that they won't be able to interview each and every star. As long as you are not rude or physical in your actions, their attention will quickly turn to the next person walking down the carpet.

While the interview is taking place, the optimal position is again behind the client, shifted off to one side, placing yourself outside of the frame of the camera. You can and should be closer than you were with the photographers, as the camera shot in interviews is usually cropped much tighter.

While your primary focus is to be scanning for threats and preparing for the unexpected, you also want to devote part of your attention to the conversation and your client's mannerisms enough to know when the interview is nearing its end. Additionally, the more seasoned protectors might actually play a part in helping to move the client along, having received a subtle cue from the protectee or the publicist that an interview is going too long or venturing into off-limit territory. A polite but firm word to the presenter (or their off-screen producer), and once again the client can save face as you are the one delivering the bad news.

FANS

The third part of the red-carpet equation are the fans. With the exception of the most reserved of events, it's really not an award show without them. They are there to bring the energy and excitement to the event, solidifying that it truly is a special night.

Unlike the first two groups of professionals (the photographers and the interviewers), and depending on the level of access and interaction with the celebrities, this section falls within the elevated risk category. The fans are chosen because they are animated and excited, and they traditionally, though not always, are in the teen to young adult range. As protectors, we must do a careful balancing act with respect for the production's desire for the celebrity to reach out and touch the fans and our mandate to provide safety.

So, unlike the two previous sections, here you need to move in very close, and no one will take offense. There are no professional photos that you need to stay out of, or televised segments to steer clear of; in fact, it's likely that the fans don't care one bit that you're even there. Chances are, they will be so wrapped up in seeing the stars in attendance that you could be waving hundred-dollar bills in front of them, and they wouldn't notice.

While it's not always possible in these settings, I strive to be closer to the protectee than the protectee is to the fans. While there is usually some type of screening process, we have to take into account the behaviors of the many fans who will be showing up hours and hours before hand to get that coveted spot in the front right next to the barricades. If it happens, it's usually the fans in the front row, and perhaps the second or third behind it, that get the opportunity to shake hands with the celebrities, and they will try to take full advantage of every moment.

In a perfect world, we would just want the VIP to wave as they are walking by; however, depending on the personality of your client, and the urgings of the production itself, they might be inclined to "press the flesh." Prior to this happening, we need to try to educate the protectee that allowing a fan to get a firm grip on them can bring harm, likely unintentional, but harm nonetheless. As cheesy as it may sound, if the VIP doesn't want to just wave, a fist-bump is the next best thing.

If you just know that the client is going to shake hands, have the client position himself further back from the barricade, so the fans have to reach all the way out and extend their arms, and not the other way around. This keeps the excited fans a little off-balance, making it more difficult to obtain a lasting grip and pull the client to them. Utilizing distance leverage and body mechanics, we give ourselves a better control of the situation versus the other way around.

For years, the ultimate expression of having made contact with the VIP was the autograph. Pen and paper were produced, and an ofttimes illegible scribble was signed by the public figure in question. Sure, some took these autographs and sold them for money, but many kept them as a memory of the rare occasion when they met their idols.

Autographs are now a thing of the past. We have all heard the old saying, "Pictures are worth a thousand words," so who wants an autograph when a photo with your favorite celebrity goes so much further in terms of social capital? These days, everyone wants a selfie, and the usual method of taking one means grabbing the star and putting an arm around them while taking the photo with the other arm. The obvious problem with this is that now a complete stranger has their arm around your client, and even with the best of intentions, bad things could happen.

To deal with this, first try to get the fan's attention verbally and visually; failing that, you can use various techniques of applying increasing pressure to the offender to cause enough discomfort for them to notice and let go. Most of the time, these individuals aren't malicious; they're just over-excited. The pressure brings their attention back out of the clouds and usually causes a correction of the behavior. With that said, in an environment like an awards show, we have to err on the side of caution and be mindful of not overdoing it. Everyone in the immediate vicinity will also have their cellphones out taking photos and video, and if you overdo the response, you are going to end up bringing the wrong kind of attention to your client's name.

My rule of thumb is that, when a fan touches the protectee (shaking a hand or grabbing an arm), you should be touching that fan. Your hand is on the fan's arm, shoulder, or small of their back, and this allows you to get their attention when you tell them that the VIP has to keep moving. Now, being in physical contact also allows you to apply pressure if needed. If there's a need to do this, remember to keep your motions and mannerisms in the realm of what a great colleague of mine, Mark James, calls "YouTube-friendly." That means, your face should project assertiveness and authority, not violence or anger. A bit of sage advice is to ask yourself, "who watches the watcher (the protector)?" The answer is everyone. Therefore, if you can see the lens, assume the lens can see you. In our contemporary world of cameras everywhere, you must keep in mind that you don't want to be replayed on the nightly news over and over for being too aggressive.

If you have a front escort, their responsibilities are to check hands and check eyes as you move along what is in essence a receiving line. Simultaneously, both you and your escort should be telling the crowd what you want and don't want them to do. "Guys and girls, I need you to have your hands out; we're not going to be posing for pictures. Sorry folks, we can't take any selfies." Keep your statements clear and concise, authoritative, but not aggressive or rude. You will be surprised that most will listen, and, after all, you can't expect them to do what they don't know.

It's likely that, after having done all three of these sections, you've now reached the end of the carpet, and what awaits is the entrance to the award show. Since only authorized persons are allowed on the carpet, it's likely that you won't be asked for a ticket, whether you have one or not. It's then time for the big show, and you are in place to provide protection as needed.

SEATING

If you get a chance to see the seats before an awards show during a site advance, you'll notice something odd: there will be cardboard place cards with photos or names peppered throughout the auditorium. These placeholders designate where the various celebrities will be seated during the event. These are important to us for several reasons. One, so we can efficiently navigate the protectee to their seat. Two, because we want to know where other VIPs of interest are seated. That's not just for trivia's sake. There could be other celebrities in proximity to our protectee who might have issues with our client, and it might be necessary for us to get our client reseated. This is particularly true in urban music, where "beefs" have a tendency of flaring up. Putting Artist A, who has a problem with Artist B, in the same row is just asking for trouble. A survey of the landscape during our advance and even a polite request to see the full seating chart can prevent these problems. Yes, you can influence the seating chart (to a degree); however, you must know how to articulate it.

In addition to the seating chart, there are specific seats marked and designated as camera seats. Think of an awards show where four people are nominated; as everyone waits in anticipation for the envelope to open, the camera magically knows where those four are sitting in a room full of hundreds, and focuses on them to get their reactions. Well, it's not magic, and not a coincidence, instead, they know who the nominees are in advance and place them in the camera seats to best capture the big moment.

Now, obviously, we as protectors don't get to determine whether our client is nominated for an award. However, camera seats matter to us because they help us figure out where we can be positioned in relation to the client. Think about it: if you know where the camera seats are, who's sitting in the seats next to them?

It should go without saying that at the major awards shows, seating is at a premium. The Grammys, the Oscars, the Emmys—for one night only, that room is THE place to be, and tickets that the celebrities receive for friends and family are extremely limited.

Even A-List talent might only receive one additional ticket in their allotment. If that is the case, that ticket usually goes to a significant other, a parent, or someone who helped them greatly in their career, like a manager or agent. So, if you don't have a ticket, and therefore don't have a seat, where do you go? The common-sense answer would be to stand in the back or along the walls of the event space, and that used to be the case many years ago.

However, with multitudes of celebrities at the show, if even a quarter of them have personal security, it would look like a football team was lined up along the side of the room. The room would feel more like a military installation than an awards show, not to mention that the fire marshal is going to have an issue with all those guys standing in the aisles. And then there's the event security itself, which is charged with the safety of the venue and its guests; just as you don't know them and their capabilities, they don't know you and yours. It's a case where no one wants to end up with egg on their face.

So, challenged with no tickets, and no place to stand, security traditionally waits in the car, or in the designated holding area, which is a separate room or structure on the grounds. At times, there are accommodations made that allow the protector to keep an eye on the proceedings via a closed-circuit feed into the room. Not an ideal situation, because it's only slightly better than being totally blind. Incidentally, because a large number of protectors end up there, the holding room can be a great place to network. However, networking isn't the reason we are there, instead, our primary responsibility is to our clients. I don't take a lot of comfort in knowing that if something happens, I'll at least have the luxury of being able to watch it on high definition TV. However, with a firm knowledge of the award show protocols, great interpersonal skills, and a bit of luck, some hidden opportunities can open up.

Let's say you have a megastar musician who's likely going to receive the Album of the Year award at the Grammys. The show itself is three hours long, and the performer and his wife brought their two young children. It's very unlikely that they are going to park themselves in their seats that entire time, knowing that that particular award won't get announced until the end of the night.

However, if they and other big stars don't come until closer to the end when they're going to get announced, there might be some noticeably empty seats for most of the evening. What if you are one of the biggest actors in the world and you are running late for the awards because of flight delays—do you think they won't let you in because the show has started? Think of a major awards show that you've seen on television. When they pan the camera on the audience, wherever direction you look, you'll notice every seat in the house is filled.

The way show producers solve the problems above is to employ specialty staff who are referred to as *seat fillers*. The name means exactly that: the role of the fillers is to make sure that there is never an empty seat in the house. Overseen by specific show producers called wranglers, the staffing is usually made up of youthful looking aspiring models from area talent agencies. These individuals are hired to look good and play the part while they sit in the seats. They are given a briefing before the show and told not to ask for any autographs or pictures or engage in any other typical "fan" behavior. With the understanding that any violation of those rules would have them ejected, and potentially blacklisted, most are on their very best behavior and are truly just happy to be there.

During a show, multiple seats come up empty on a frequent basis for a variety of reasons, sometimes because a star hasn't arrived yet, other times because he or she has gone backstage to get ready to present or perform. When this happens, fillers are dispatched from their holding area and quickly move into those empty spots.

So how do we use this information and make it work for us? Let's say the client and his agent have tickets for two seats in the second row. If the agent isn't in the seat right now, who is? A seat filler. The savvy protector who understands the process will walk up to the seat filler and firmly (but politely) ask them to get up. Remember, they are there to serve a purpose—to look presentable and act the part; you could also fulfill that same role. What that does mean is that you can't look like you just walked out of the gym or rolled out of bed, instead, you have to be dressed appropriately and blend in. For most award shows, the preferred attire is formal, and while you don't necessarily need to be in a tuxedo, a basic dark suit would fit the bill. However, the key word here is basic, as there are many different types of suit styles, cuts, lengths, and fits. So, if you look like you just stepped out of the movie, *Saturday Night Fever,* or if you don't know how to correctly tie a half

Windsor, then I suggest you practice to proficiency, or invest in a nice clip-on. For female protectors, the order of the day is to wear something sleek enough to look like you belong, while at the same time remaining operational.

That also means that you need to leave the "ice grill" at the door. (For those who don't know, that's slang for angry scowl.) The show producers don't want the viewing audience to see some menacing guys obviously scanning in the audience. This is one of the occasions where we would intentionally soften our hard exterior and be more welcoming and accommodating, as this is a role we need to play to exist in this space.

Now, the ability for you as a protector to be able to assume the seat filler role isn't a foolproof system, and it's not going to work 100 percent of the time. To ensure better chances of success, you need to have developed a relationship with the production staff. These are the men and women who run the show, and theirs is often a thankless and stressful job. Everyone wants or needs something, and they are under extreme amounts of pressure, particularly on event day. Develop a rapport, don't be pushy, and you will likely find that they can make magic happen for you.

Over time, you will be able to identify seat fillers pretty quickly, and should be able to recognize many of the marquee-level VIPs (I mean, they are potential clients after all). As a savvy protector, you will be paying attention to the production staff scurrying around, also identifiable by their radios, earpieces, and clipboards. From there, you'll be able to identify the wranglers, as you'll see them scan their seating chart whenever there is an open seat and quickly direct someone into it.

Having personally done this dance many times, I can now just walk up to the seat filler and say, "Hey, I need that seat," and they gladly oblige. Remember they are just happy to be there, are used to being moved around, plus they have no idea who you are. One word of caution: do this with extreme tact and take great care to make sure you don't tell a VIP's spouse or significant other to move. Recognizable celebrities are not the only VIPs at award shows, so you have to be extremely careful with this method. A safer starting point is identifying a wrangler and mention that you gave your seat up to a VIP and ask if they wouldn't mind placing you in a filler seat, also adding that you'd be happy to move again if needed.

If your client is the recipient of an award that night, they will likely be seated in a camera seat. Those are often located near the end of the aisle so that, when their name is announced, they'll have easy access to the aisle, and can make it to the stage with minimal bustle and stepping over people. In a perfect world, you would want to be sitting closest to the aisle, but in this case, you will likely have an inside seat. When the announcement is made, stay seated so you're not disrupting the shot. After the protectee gets up and the camera follows them onstage, you then have time to move from your seat to the backstage area, where they will be directed to after they give their acceptance speech, for photos, interviews, or to prep for a performance.

Effectively handling big nights like this is what can cement your position as a Tier 1 protector in the celebrity sector. The clients, their representatives, and the production staff will notice the difference between how you operate versus other who don't have your understanding of the protocols. The added bonus is that there is a lot of crossover with production companies and personnel, meaning that many of the individuals and entities that put on one major event are the same people that put on another. So, once you have fostered those relationships and they realize that you know what you're doing, it will get easier and easier and you will gain more and more access. Conversely, if you don't know what you're doing, if you're in the way, or always in the photos, someone in authority is inevitably going to ask you to go wait in the car, and that's going to make for a long night.

Chapter 10

EVENT SECURITY

EVENT SECURITY STAFF

The headline read, "Mariah Carey's Bodyguard Accused of Beating a Fan." The next line, also in large print, quoted an individual on the scene: "All I did is film him attacking a fan and he grabbed my phone and started punching me."

However, when the actual facts of the story started to emerge, Mariah Cary's representative said no members of her security team were involved in the scuffle but the responsible person was actually a part of the venue event security staff.[1]

Most people can pick out security event staff fairly quickly: they are the ones responsible for public admission and building security during an event. They usually wear uniform jackets or shirts emblazoned with the words *Event Security, Staff,* or *Security* on the back. A large majority of them fall into the demographic of students, housewives, or retirees, having little or no training in actual physical security. They may or may not possess a security guard license and even fewer would have taken any type of security-related course or exam. What they have been, is orientated into the rules and procedures of the venue, and enforcement of those remain their primary objective. They have no authority of arrest, but hold responsibility for assuring the safe movement of people and security of the building and event. Many event venues hire security on a regular basis and, as private employers, there may be little to no additional or continuous training aside from what is received on the job.

---

1. Retrieved 1/31/18 from aceshowbiz.com/news/view/00116259.html

The challenge then becomes how do we effectively conduct our assignments when we have no idea of the level of training or commitment we will receive from the venue side? Compounding that is the reality that, if something goes wrong, it is the artist and the artist's personal security who will likely be blamed.

PLACEMENT

In terms of placement, when I work with musician clients who are performing onstage, the challenge is to figure out how to be close enough to be effective, but not so close that you are interfering with the aesthetics of the show. I have found the most advantageous position to be either stage right or stage left, outside of the public's view but with a clear line of sight to the protectee.

Once you have done this a while, you will notice that, for the majority of entertainers, the performance is usually the same with only small variations night after night. In fact, after a while, you might be able to perform the whole show in your head, having seen and heard it so many times. Due to that repetition, it would be very easy to tune out, to mentally drift away and lose focus—but rest assured that when that happens is precisely when Murphy's Law again will pay a visit.

On one occasion at a festival show, a stage crasher somehow made it onto the stage by evading the venue security lined up in the pit in front. He then scaled the seven-foot high scaffolding before emerging from an area to the side of the stage. Broadcasting the performance to the thousands in attendance was a huge video screen, which also provided cover for me to be close to the stage by standing behind it. The disadvantage to the screen was that it obstructed my vision directly to its front, and it was with that setup that I didn't see the stage crasher until he ran into my field of view, making a direct beeline to the client. Fortunately, I was able to intercept him as he made his way to the protectee from behind. Once I had him I quickly hustled him off the stage and turned him over to other members of the security staff so I could get back into position with my eyes on the protectee. The incident occurred so quickly that the client had no idea it even happened until later when it hit the media, having been captured and broadcast by the scores of audience-goers in attendance.

Now, if this individual had reached the client, could I say, "Hey, that wasn't my fault; the festival producers put these big video screens here?" Could I say, "Hey, that wasn't my fault; we're seven feet in the air and we have venue security whose job is to keep people off the stage?" Yes, I could have said these things, but it wouldn't count for anything. As the primary protector, we are ultimately responsible for the client's safety, and that requires staying in the moment, even when there are other layers of security in place.

Our role is more than just standing at a door or walking the client to a car. We have to handle logistics; we have to be thinking about the next step and—this is the important part—we have to be able to respond quickly and decisively when something happens. I could have done everything right that whole day, and if this individual who jumped up on the stage were to have reached the client in front of thirty thousand people, the rest wouldn't matter.

Alternatively, if a guy jumps on the stage and I dropkick him and beat him senseless in front of all those people and the cameras, the client and I could easily end up with a different kind of problem, usually in the form of a lawsuit. Our mission is to protect not only the clients' physical person, but also their brand.

CREDENTIALS: LIMITING AND CONTROLLING ACCESS

In my opinion, many in our profession don't pay as much attention to credentials as they need to. They just go with the flow, and figure that the venue takes care of credentials, so it's not their problem. However, if you understand the process and can influence the process, it will make your life easier in the long run. You can increase your chances of success and minimize the chances of anyone disrupting the system, at least long enough for you to get your client in and out of that particular environment.

Credentials are necessary to both *limit* access and *control* access. Limited access means that if you don't have credentials, you simply can't gain entry. Controlling access means that specific credentials allow only certain individuals in pre-established areas, while other credentials might be valid only in other areas.

In essence, just having a pass doesn't mean a person can go everywhere; however, the issue is that many times, just because someone has something hanging around their neck, event staff, including security, will just wave them on through. Of course, this defeats the purpose of having the credentials in the first place, and it is for this reason that we must be able to influence the pass protocol and have a measure of comfort in the training and assertiveness of the event staff.

At a performance event, two types of passes are at play: the artist passes and the venue passes, with the latter usually created by the individual venue and therefore being different at each location. While we as protectors will usually have minimal input on the venue passes, we should play a part in the creation of the artist pass. Depending on how well you can insert yourself into the process, that can range from providing input such as recommending a holographic foil or photo, to actually being responsible for designing the pass from top to bottom and then submitting it for client approval.

The unfortunate reality is that most passes are ripe for counterfeiting these days. Almost anyone in the general public has access to high-quality copiers and printers; combine that with a little skill in Photoshop and you have the makings of a security nightmare. With that in mind, we have to make sure we stay at least one step ahead of counterfeiters by creating the passes using materials that are difficult to duplicate. Some suggestions for multiday events include making each pass specific to the date via color coding. You can also number the passes, adding the specific person's name and photo on it as an even higher level of security. I personally am a big fan of the number/photo system, as it allows us to immediately match the pass to the person/department, which is especially useful in larger productions involving lots of people.

Artist passes should also include different subsets; for example, one type for talent, one for production, one for management, and so forth. These distinctions can be minimal, but they allow the staff to quickly determine if the right person is in the right place.

Passes usually are divided into two main categories, *hard* and *soft*. Hard passes take the form of laminates, which, as the name implies, are laminated plastic over cardstock. They are a bit sturdier and are intended for repeat use. Soft passes are temporary stick-ons or wristbands, usually made of a satin material with artwork printed on one side. These are designed for one-time use, say for Artist Meet & Greets, media, or giving friends and family after-show access.

Passes within the same event might be a combination of different colors and shapes, combining laminates, stickies, and wristbands.

To keep track of the different pass types and what type of access each one allows, there will need to be the creation of a pass sheet. If you're running the operation, you will need to produce a master pass sheet; if you are a part of a larger production, someone else will be in charge of its creation, and you will be informed of the details so you know what's needed for your client and entourage to move around with minimal hassle.

The pass sheet should be distributed to both artist security and venue security. While shielded from the general public, it should also be posted in access control areas so that key personnel can quickly glance at, or refer to, the sheet for people entering that particular zone.

COMMON TYPES OF PASSES

FOH

This stands for Front of House, a production workspace usually located on or near the general public event floor. Because of the equipment, this area will need to be secured via access control.

Escort VIP Pass Only

This is a one-time pass given to someone who, by nature of their credential, can escort a VIP guest.

Backstage with Escort

Let's say the band's drummer wants to bring his significant other to the show. The only way he can bring her backstage is to have a pass that allows her to be there, provided that she is escorted by him. This would work in conjunction with his pass.

All Access, FOH, No Escort Privileges

The most common pass for individuals directly involved with the production (artist, band, management, etc.), this traditionally takes the form of a hard laminate. A soft version of this pass may be available for a limited duration; for example, if an executive from the record label is in town to see the show. This pass will give them freedom of movement, but it prevents them from bringing guests of their own backstage and is good for a limited amount of time only.

All Access, Full Escort

This is essentially translated as, "Do not hinder, do not impede." This pass includes all of the privileges listed above, with the ability to also escort others into restricted areas. This pass would be among the rarest, distributed to individuals such as the security detail leader, artist management, or others involved at senior levels in running the show.

Press Pit Only

Simply having a nice camera isn't reason enough to gain entry into the press pit; instead, authorized personnel will need to have this official credential. This pass is usually valid for a limited duration (example: 3–4 songs) and does not allow access backstage by itself. Case in point, you don't want photographers capturing the client walking around in a robe and hair rollers before getting dressed for the show.

Working Pass

This is usually a temporary satin for venue staff who are interacting with the production in an official capacity. For example, the union workhands who assist the touring crew in setting up and tearing down the stage would receive this pass.

Stage Worker

This pass is the same as the Working Pass, but with stage access; something to take notice of, as your protectee will be on that stage at some point.

LIMITING PASSES

In regards to issuing passes, it's important to make sure that everybody who needs one has one. With that said, one of the most vital parts of access control is limiting the number of passes issued. The best pass systems have built-in accountability with repercussions for losing them.

In regards to counterfeit passes, we have to keep in mind that people are always going to be trying to circumvent the system. That is why the more you are involved in the credentialing process, the better you'll be able to limit and control access, and the better you'll be able to deal with people who try to get around those controls.

Sometimes, fake passes can start out innocently enough; for example, someone who holds a legitimate pass just can't resist posting a photo of their pass on social media during the show. However, what that does is make it possible for someone else to get creative in making a copy of that pass with their own photo on it. That pass image taken with just about any cell phone these days can be downloaded, copied, and manipulated to look just as legitimate as the original.

A few years back, there was a young man who gained access to the NBA All-Star game despite all of the security put in place at a major event like that. Calling it an "experiment," he found a photo of the press pass for the game, printed it out and had it laminated at a local copy place. He purchased a fancy holder like the ones that journalists and convention-goers wear. To seal the deal, he put on his best dark suit, and just like that, he was pretty much given All-Access to the game.

To document his accomplishment, he took photos near the court, backstage in the locker room, and even of the game trophy. In this instance, this individual wasn't trying to do anyone any harm, but think about what could have happened if he did want to cause harm or embarrassment to the players, the managers, or the fans. I leave security out of that "what if" statement because, intended or not, I'm sure those professionals were embarrassed by the breach when it made the social media rounds. Remember, access control has to be a shared responsibility that everyone is vested in.

BACKSTAGE CRASHERS

Backstage crashers will generally look like they know what they are doing, and will often attempt to find an access point based on wherever they think the weakest link is. The skilled ones will ignore security, walking around as if they own the place, projecting confidence, so that most people assume they belong.

Backstage crashers will do their best to stay out of the way and keep moving, floating around from place to place so people become comfortable seeing them, but never remaining in one spot where someone might question their role or function. Essentially, they hide in plain sight.

These individuals are rarely fans (in their own minds, that is); instead, when confronted, they always have a different reason as to why they were backstage. This could be attributed to them just lying after getting caught, but it may be their own psychology, which has them actually believe that they need to be around celebrities and partake in their world. These types of crashers often feel some conflict; while they are excited that they have circumvented the system, they also feel guilty that they had to resort to such means to do it.

THE FESTIVAL CRASHER

Monitoring credentials and backstage access is tough at music festivals, both because of the sheer size of the large events, and because many of the security staff are inexperienced and undertrained. I can recall an occasion at an outdoor festival in which the restricted backstage area was created by forming a semi-circle using the artists' trailers. This allowed for a sizable grassy area in which the various performers and credentialed staff could lounge around and prepare for the show prior to their appointed time on stage.

With my protectee inside his trailer, and me stationed in front of the door, I noticed two gentlemen walk past; one of them had a visible credential, but the other did not. The protocol was that everyone in this area would have been vetted by the event security at the entrance to the circle, so once this individual came near our trailer, I thought it was important to ask him if he could display his credential. After he replied that he didn't have it with him, I mentioned that to be in this area, he was required to have a pass on display at all times.

He then tried to convince me that everything was okay by passing me a business card. The card itself looked interesting to say the least; for starters, the company name and logo stated *Universal Music Group Italy*, with this individual listed as a Vice President. However, curiously enough, under the company name was a UK address, as opposed to an Italian one. In addition, under the individual's name, it listed an American street address accompanied by a Yahoo email address, pretty unusual for someone that high up the corporate ladder.

As I looked at the card and at the man, I had this feeling that he did seem familiar somehow, but not necessarily in a good way. While I couldn't place him at first, I then remembered an article I had read some time before about a man arrested on suspicion of misdemeanor and criminal trespassing—by way of false credentials, at another very high-profile music show, and this sounded like the same hustle.

So, with his card in hand, I did a quick online search on my phone, pulled up the news story from the year before, and lo and behold, it was the same person, confirmed via his mugshot in the paper, and here he was, at it again.

I then walked him over to the event security and asked that he be removed from the premises. During this process, he didn't offer any rationale or even attempt to explain the charade. As my primary responsibility was elsewhere, I just needed the assurance that he would be removed and not allowed to reenter the secure area. After his expulsion, I again spoke with the guard at the security checkpoint who allowed him entry in the first place. Upon inquiring how that happened, his response was, "Why wouldn't I let him in? This is *his* show."

Apparently, days before the official start of the festival, the gate crasher started coming around and introducing himself to the construction workers and security staff and giving out his card. By the time the actual show day came around, everybody recognized him and thought not only that he belonged, but that he was one of the senior event organizers and therefore didn't need credentials.

To this day, I still can't tell you what his motivation was. I don't know if he's a music fan (it was a different festival, and a different line-up of artists), or if he's got some underlying issues that need to be worked out. It couldn't simply be because he wanted to avoid paying, because he had already gained entry into the show. Whatever his motivation, these are the kinds of people that we have to always be watching out for, again proving that our job is more than just standing idly at a door.

SECURING THE STAGE

It might seem like a given, but our responsibility to our client doesn't end when they hit the stage. While we might securely control the backstage area, that isn't the only place that could be breached.

Depending on the height of the stage, an exuberant (and likely inebriated) fan might, accidentally or otherwise, try to jump onto the stage or pull the protectee off. Even with the most innocent of intentions, the excitement of the moment might cause fans to try and grab for anything within reach that belongs to the protectee—including limbs, clothing, and jewelry.

Good security involves multiple layers, concentric rings of protection that together allow us to harden the target. Determined fans (or an attacker) can sometimes make it through one or more layers, but the purpose of multiple layers of security is to prevent those fans or attackers from reaching the VIP.

Whenever possible, we as the primary protector want to maintain close proximity to our client, yet this presents a problem during show time because, traditionally speaking, we want to avoid being on the stage and therefore be seen as part of the show. Similar to the red-carpet events, the goal is maintaining proximity to the protectee without sticking out like a sore thumb. As mentioned earlier, I have found that the optimal position for the bodyguard is onstage in the wings, positioned either stage right or stage left. Exactly which side is usually determined by a variety of factors, such as line of sight, obstacles and obstructions, and the backstage egress points. Remember, if we have to move the client off the stage, rarely are we just going to stop there, so where we are retreating to in an emergency also plays a part.

If the client is interacting with the audience, say shaking hands with fans at the end of the show, in most situations you can justify being on the actual stage. Your role would be similar to fan interaction during red carpet events, making sure the protectee isn't pulled off-balance, and verbalizing what you want the fans to do or not do, in a firm but not overly aggressive manner. For example, "Guys, just wave. Don't push," and so forth.

Note: depending on the performer/performance, this might not be an option at all. Some artists are very particular about their stage, and if you aren't singing, dancing, or playing an instrument, they don't want you there. If that's the case, improvise and adapt. Just prior to the curtain call, you might want to position yourself or one of your agents in the pit or actually embedded in the first few rows of the floor so you can respond from that direction if necessary.

Ultimately, while the client is onstage, we need to be able to simultaneously stand out and blend in. We need to be extremely observant of not only the artist, but the crowds and the positioning of the support security. We need to be able to react if needed, but not OVERreact, which could have career-ending consequences. No one said it would be easy.

SIGNING SESSIONS

Celebrity protectees need to relate to their fans, and one way they do that is in autograph signing sessions. At these sessions, they can have more personal interactions with their fanbase while at the same time promoting and selling whatever their latest product is. In theory, it's a match made in heaven; however, it can be a source of anxiety and frustration for protectors if not handled right.

Protective measures for the client doing signing sessions need to begin well before the pen (or sharpie) touches the paper. Those fans that line up around the block, camping out for hours and even days, need direction. Where do they stand? Will they block traffic or other area businesses? What's the plan for inclement weather? Sure, the venue might bear the brunt of the responsibility for figuring this out, but ultimately, if something goes wrong, it's the client's brand that is damaged. Proactive protectors will integrate themselves into the process early, offering input and planning for contingencies.

Don't underestimate the fact that logistics will play a major part—how will you get in, and how will you get out? Remember, in many cases, those fans are lined up around the building, so choose your entrance and exit routes carefully.

Depending on the size of the venue and the level of interaction, additional resources may be needed, and if those resources can't come in the form of trained close protection agents, it will be up to you to make sure that the venue's staff is up to speed on your expectations. Remember, we want them to be alert and on their toes, but we also must take care to make sure that they don't overdo it. The excitement or pressure of the moment sometimes causes security staff to overreact, and that can create additional headaches that no one wants.

Once you have the extra help, then you need to decide where to place them; that might mean adding front and rear escorts, and for larger crowds, or signings in sketchier areas, possibly law enforcement.

One useful tactic is to incorporate the environment into your security plan; in the case of a signing at a store, this can be in the form of using the furnishings to create barriers. I am a firm believer that if you can use a natural barricade (e.g., a feature in the store) it looks better than an artificial one. At a music store, see about the possibility of re-purposing the CD racks to create aisles and dead ends, funneling the traffic in the direction you intend. Think how you would make it function like a TSA airport line would, but in an organic way, created by props native to the environment.

If you have the choice in setting up the room, another good tip is to have the table on a raised platform. This creates separation without looking like that's the intent, and if anyone below tries to do something disruptive, they are going to have additional ground to cover.

Having a table also allows for the client to sit, reducing fatigue, especially if it's going to be a long signing. It also has the added value of discouraging posed photos with fans. While, tactically speaking, it's easier to move the protectee standing instead of sitting, if you can make sure the seat is a rolling chair and things get out of control, just roll them right on out of the area!

Try to set up the signing so that you have control over the entrance and exits into the room, ideally with the client having a different ingress and egress point than the attendees. There will need to be an access control point at the entry to vet the authorized attendees and prevent those that will try and sneak or con their way in. Some signing sessions are for product that isn't out yet, so recording devices like phones might need to be prohibited. While you may or may not choose to run the fans through metal detectors, it's reasonable to have them open their bags for a visual inspection.

Give some thought to how many people are in line and how long each fan can have with the protectee given the time available. If you have 400 people, how long is the signing going to take if the client spends an average of 30 seconds per person? A signing such as this is going to run over three hours and that's if everything flows smoothly. You'll also need to factor in time for breaks for the protectee as they might get hungry or need the restroom facilities. You may wonder why we would need to concern ourselves with this as it sounds like something management or the venue would shepherd along. Again, the more integrated you are into the process, the more control you have to ensure that nothing goes wrong from a safety or security point of view, and that no harm is done to the client's image.

If there's one thing that will disrupt the flow, that would be allowing the fans to use their own cameras or phones to take photos, so whenever possible, that should be avoided. Instead, suggest to management that they should provide their own photographers who can have the shot in focus and captured quickly. At the end of the line, the fans receive a card with the website address where they can download the photo, and the line keeps moving.

You will want to balance safety with accessibility, but in doing so, you will find it tougher at a signing session to remain closer to the protectee than the protectee is to the public. Again, most clients don't want to look like they have or need overwhelming security surrounding them at all times. One way to get around this is to become more involved in the meet and greet process. Think about the visual signals you are sending: perhaps this occasion could take you out of your normal suit and tie and find you dressing more casually so that you fit in. If it's a two-agent team, having the second agent in a suit draws a distinction, and now you have the best of both worlds. A casual observer will think that that guy is the security, and when they see you, they'll just assume that you are one of the venue staff or part of the client's management team.

For example, let's say the event is a CD signing, and you want to adhere to the Arm's Length Away philosophy. You as the bodyguard don't look quite so imposing if you dress down, so now it's possible that from the front of the table, you could handle the task of directing the line of people up to the receiving table and asking the fans to open up their CDs. This allows you to control the speed and flow of the crowd, and also provides you the opportunity to give clear directions to the fans, all while being in a position that puts you in an effective range to respond to problems.

Oftentimes fans will request a hug, and there are occasions when the client will oblige. While not encouraged, that is a reality of dealing with celebrities and their fans. With that said, every time someone is touching the protectee, we want to make sure that we are positioned where we can reach out and touch that individual. This way, if we need to prompt them with a light tap or apply a little bit of pressure for the overly zealous to remember to let go, they'll get the message pretty quickly. Keeping a neutral expression or even a smile on your face while you do so ensures that it's YouTube-friendly—which is important, as there are likely tons of cameras around.

Chapter 11

WORKING WITH THE MEDIA

DEALING WITH PAPARAZZI AND PREVENTING EMBARRASSMENT

Working with celebrity clients inevitably means that you're going to be working with the media in some way, shape, or form. As this is the case, you have to be ever-mindful that while you are protecting your client physically, you also have a mandate to protect their image.

Gone are the days when celebrities could be anonymous, appearing only on the stage, silver screen, or red carpet and then disappearing into the ether until their next project. These days, every aspect of their personal lives is broadcast, dissected, and talked about on social media without end. The driving factor behind this is what I have termed The Rise of The Blogs and the 24-hour News Cycle. Those of us with more than a few decades under our belt will recall that there was a time when broadcast news used to come on just three times a day: early in the morning, during dinner, and at night before bed. For that matter, television itself used to end in the late-night hours, with a final broadcast of the flag and some patriotic music playing before the entire station faded into static.

Then cable television appeared and took the world by storm, and since customers were paying up front for the service, advertising revenues from commercials weren't needed. Additionally, to appeal to the widest consumer base possible, there was no need for programming to end; it could just go on and on with one day bleeding into the next. CNN was one of the first news outlets to meet (or some would argue, create) the demands of the subscribers and offer 24 hours of round-the-clock news.

At first, actual news is what you got, but the reality is, there is only so much happening any given day, and yet producers still had open timeslots to fill within those 24 hours of every day. They then started regurgitating the news, offering replays or alternative takes of stories they had already covered that day, but there are only so many times you can hear the same story *ad infinitum*. Therefore, in the never-ending quest to find news stories, the definition of what was "news" started to change. Stories that were once suitable only for supermarket tabloids, such as what a celebrity was wearing today, or who she was dating, started being placed right alongside world-changing events, all in an effort to feed the 24-hour beast. This subsequently led to the mainstreaming of the paparazzi and their increased efforts to document all things celebrity.

The other factor involved here is the blogs, online websites that pretty much existed only as a small subgroup until about 15 years ago. Originally, celebrity-related blogs consisted mainly of text, and were used as a place to dish up the latest happenings of celebrities to their readers, much the way a gossip column would in a lifestyle magazine. With advancements in technology, the blog owners realized that if they added photos to their blogs, they would draw more traffic to their websites—traffic that would convert into revenue for the site owner.

The truth of the matter is, the main reason that most commercial blogs exist today is to make money, and they do that by selling advertising on their pages. Now, the way to draw more advertisers in, and justify and command certain advertising rates, is to get more traffic to their sites. Traffic is essentially the viewers who go to any given web page to read the stories, and who could see, and potentially click, on the ads that are displayed there. Bloggers were then faced with the same dilemma as network news: they needed more and more content to get people to keep returning to their sites.

Proving that the old saying is true, they began to realize that it's easier to use pictures than to have to come up with pages and pages of text and stories that were engaging enough to read. Alternatively, photos had a powerful chance of drawing the viewers in, and more consumers were looking at photos and videos online now that bandwidth was becoming more and more affordable. They then noticed that if a picture of a famous actress going into Starbucks gave them a certain number of hits (individuals stopping by the site), if that same actress did the same thing, but this time the photographer captured a shot of her just as the wind lifted up her dress, there was a dramatic increase in viewership and therefore potential ad revenue.

This led to site owners looking and paying not just for celebrity photos, but specifically *embarrassing* celebrity photos, because those were proven to generate more traffic. The problem for the paparazzi who were in the business of snapping and selling the photos was that the odds of any given actress stepping over a subway vent just as she went into a restaurant were pretty slim. So, they then began creating situations where the celebrity would be likely to do something embarrassing, aggressive, or out of the norm. This way, they could then capture the moment and sell it to the blog for the higher rate. The blog would then put it up for the world to see, generating more hits and therefore more potential ad revenue.

This is the reason the paparazzi exist in this day and age and why they continue to be such a problem for celebrities and their bodyguards. However, if you don't understand the business model that they and the publications they work for are following, you won't know how to successfully interact and deal with them. The other things the blogs are full of is documented cases of bodyguards who don't get this, and instead overreact with the paparazzi and end up jeopardizing their careers.

PRESS VERSUS PAPARAZZI

While the lines between them may be blurring a bit, historically, the difference between the press and the paparazzi boils down to two words: journalistic integrity. The press is at least supposed to adhere to the codes of journalistic integrity, whereas the paparazzi, on the other hand, don't pledge themselves to any codes of conduct. For example, if you're talking to a journalist and clearly state that something is "off the record," and they agree to that, following their code of ethics, they are not supposed to write that down.

On the other hand, if you're dealing with the paparazzi and you say that something is off the record, no matter how many assurances they give you, it will likely get published, and it's the same with photos. The paparazzi are out to take whatever they can get, with or without permission, in whatever quantity they want, because they're not bothered by that little thing called *journalistic integrity*. Knowing they lack this, our mission is to figure out how to best deal with them.

If a celebrity entering an airport gets a microphone stuck in his face and his response is, "Don't talk to me," you know what the paparazzi are going to do—keep talking. Think about it, if they can get under the client's skin, even better. Remember, the average picture would just show him going into the airport—a pretty humdrum shot for the blogs, one that would translate into low clicks. But if the paps can provoke the VIP (or their security) into losing their cool, all of a sudden, they have something noteworthy and of increased value.

But why are celebrity clients so bent out of shape about the paparazzi, requesting no pictures at even the most public of outings, and even going so far as to get verbally and even physically aggressive? The reason most celebrity clients don't want their pictures taken is surprisingly simple: it's because they don't get any revenue off of those photos. For example, back in the day, if you wanted a picture of Michael Jackson, you went to the concession stand at the concert and you paid $20 for a poster, and a portion of those retail sales went to the King of Pop. Nowadays, celebrities don't get money from the scores of photos captured by the paps, sold to the blogs, and reposted on hundreds of other sites.

In this new digital, instant information age, the celebrities have found that they can't control their likeness. Where they used to be able to monetize their image and enforce their trademark, these days, everybody has a smart phone; with one push of a button, the information is released onto the world wide web, never to return.

Recall, as bodyguards, we're supposed to protect both the client and their image, and that includes not letting the paparazzi bait us into doing anything that could be considered assault or theft. Sometimes, in our zeal to adhere to the client's wishes, we end up creating bigger problems with exponentially bigger consequences.

Several years ago, a disturbing video surfaced of a bodyguard for a very famous actress being followed by the paparazzi. In the video, you can see the bodyguard pull over, get out and, after an exchange of words, end up beating the cameraman badly, all while the photographer has the video camera running.

At the end of the video, we see the protector walking away followed by the driver taking the camera and turning it to capture his bloodied and bruised face. This is called the *money shot*, because an incident that had little to no value before (a celebrity in a car) will now pay huge dividends in the form of a lawsuit.

Now it's very possible that the actress said to her protector that she didn't want any photos—again, the underlining issue is that celebrities do not make any money from the video or pictures anymore, and they tire of the endless harassment the photographers employ to get the shot. However, if her quest was for anonymity, it backfired to a disastrous degree. In the end, the headlines both in print and online talked about how her bodyguard beat up this innocent photographer. Incidentally, the bodyguard's name was rarely mentioned in the coverage, and was never mentioned in the headline. The lawsuit was reportedly in the millions, and if the aim was to protect the client's image, the result was the polar opposite.

In another infamous video, the bodyguard of a very well-known celebrity can be overheard saying to a throng of paparazzi, "Anybody in my way is going to get pushed." All that did was tell the paparazzi that the money shot would come from doing exactly that, namely, getting in his way.

On this particular occasion, the VIP was leaving a dentist's office, and she can be viewed in the footage covering her face with a sweater. While it's possible that the client's face may have been swollen from a dental procedure, it's equally likely that she just did not want to be filmed, since she would not be compensated for the use of her image. So, with the paparazzi crowding, and the protector about to head to the car with his client, assistance came in the unusual form of the building maintenance man. He proceeded to open an umbrella to hide the celebrity's face, while the bodyguard walked his client through the crowd, trying to shield her. However, the umbrella wasn't only hiding the VIP's face; it also obstructed the bodyguard's line of sight.

Recall what the bodyguard said: "Anybody in my way is going to get pushed." Naturally, the paparazzi made every effort to be in the way as the bodyguard moved the client to the vehicle. One solid groin kick later, and a photographer is screaming in pain. Additionally, the client can also be heard on tape wincing in pain, because the agent did that kick while still holding on to her, causing her to twist her ankle.

So instead of protecting, the bodyguard actually ended up injuring his client, and we know all of this because the other paparazzi in attendance happily filmed the whole scene, including the money shot with the kick and the ankle-twisting. You can imagine the other paparazzi in attendance would likely line up to testify on behalf of their brother-in-arms if called upon.

In the end, the photographer sued, for a reported amount of $250,000. Keep in mind that this all originated from the client wanting to protect her image. But instead of an uninteresting photo of a celebrity leaving an office, which would have been of very low value, the choices that the protector made potentially ended up costing a quarter of a million dollars, not to mention being viewed on YouTube over one million times on just a single site. Negative publicity from the headlines aside, that's a lot of page views, which translate into ad revenue that the VIP sees none of. In essence, the result was the total opposite of what she was trying to accomplish.

My final example comes in the form of a megastar musician who was exiting a jewelry store with his security detail. Once they were outside, the paparazzi quickly swarmed, and while I can only guess what was going through the mind of the protector in the front escort position, I'll give him the benefit of the doubt and assume that he got startled. The protector punched one of the paparazzi, knocking him to the ground, and as he fell, the other cameramen on the scene took a quick series of shots documenting his fall in high definition all the way down to the concrete. Click-click-click-click-click.

The photographer sued for 14 million dollars. He said that he hurt his head impacting the sidewalk, and that he injured his back striking the curb. In his civil suit alleging physical and emotional distress, he outlined his now frequent headaches, and went so far as to say that he can no longer listen to music, amongst a list of other physical and psychological ailments. So, for all of this pain and suffering caused at the hands of the VIP and his protector, he wanted the court to award him millions of dollars.

Regardless of what they settled for in the court proceedings, at the end of the day, no shot the paparazzi would have captured would have been worth a fraction of that amount. In the end, we have to make sure that we do not fall into the traps set by these cameramen. They have a job to do, and while ours puts us on the opposite of the game board, we have to treat our responses more like chess than checkers. If you can educate your client into the thought process and motivations of the paparazzi beforehand, they will find that instead of jumping them, you can win by sacrificing a pawn (a photo) to prevent a Queen or King-sized lawsuit.

Chapter 12

ADDITIONAL CONSIDERATIONS

LAW ENFORCEMENT VERSUS PROTECTIVE SERVICES

There are valuable similarities yet distinct differences between law enforcement duties and protective services. For example, a sworn police officer is trained to help anyone and everyone needing assistance as well as provide security to society as a whole. Conversely, personal protectors provide services to a very narrowly defined specific person or group. A police officer is reactive by nature, responding to incidents he observes or is dispatched to; in contrast, by and large, the bodyguard is proactive, providing preplanned, even rehearsed, security and movements of the person being protected.

Law enforcement has the power and duty of arrest for crimes observed; a protector has no similar responsibility or power, and any detention or arrest he or she makes becomes a citizen's arrest with the inherent obligations of filing a complaint and pursuing prosecution. A police officer represents the authority of the city or state and is protected from liability when acting in an official capacity; the bodyguard has no more authority than an average citizen and is responsible for any liability they may incur.

The police function is most distinct when it is high profile, like driving clearly identifiable vehicles, wearing a uniform with a visible badge and equipment belt holding his weapon, handcuffs, communications, and so forth. A personal protection person or team traditionally blends in more to their protectee's lifestyle, usually minimizing drawing attention to themselves and being nonconfrontational unless there is no other option.

SIMILARITIES

Both law enforcement and personal protectors prevent specific criminal acts against individuals in their sphere of influence. They investigate threats. Both gather intelligence and make threat assessments, and both detect threats, risks. and vulnerabilities.

They both aim to deter any adverse action and respond to emergencies. Both have restrictions on the use of force, which is limited to reasonable and necessary use (i.e., only if life is in immediate danger).

Both must be knowledgeable in current news events and trends, good public relations, security procedures and laws, protocol, emergency medical procedures and crisis recognition. And both must maintain professional conduct.

DISENGAGEMENT

Bodyguards, like law enforcement officers, are often placed in circumstances that, if not handled correctly, could easily escalate to violence or the necessary use of force. The position of bodyguard is required to be nonconfrontational unless there is no other option. The clear primary objective is to de-escalate the moment.

In terms of de-escalation, there are several things to avoid. You don't want to threaten the aggressor with violence or make other threats. Don't perpetuate the argument by contradicting the aggressor, particularly with your protectee in the immediate vicinity. Don't challenge the aggressor by getting in their face or by calling them names,[1] and don't shame or disrespect the aggressor. If your goal is de-escalation, do not lay hands on the aggressor.

One of the most important skills when attempting to de-escalate a crisis is communication. When appropriate to the situation, establish dialogue with these techniques:

- Break the ice. This will help the subject initiate dialogue and establish rapport. Basic conversational things like introducing yourself can help accomplish this.

---

1. Rivera, Luis. De-escalation: The Art of Avoiding Violence. Retrieved 09/16/17 from endesastres.org/files/The_best_way_to_deal_with_violence_is_to_avoid_it_1_.pdf

- Listen for the total meaning of the words spoken by the individual—this is critical in establishing dialogue.
- Help provide reflecting statements—use minimal encouragers like. . . . "I can see why you are so displeased." Minimal encouragers are short responses that let the other person know he or she is being listened to; use comments such as, "I hear you, got it, I'm with you."
- Using "I" statements, restating statements, reflecting, and summarizing or paraphrasing are all techniques that been proven effective by de-briefers and psychologists specialized in crisis negotiation situations and isolating events.
- Remember that communication is not an individual sport. For communication to be effective, it must afford both parties the ability to exchange information. This exchange must create a climate of mutual understanding. The bottom line is that to be able to communicate effectively, one must be an active listener. Active listening requires the listener to understand, interpret, and evaluate what they hear. The ability to listen actively can improve personal relationships through reducing conflicts, strengthening cooperation, and fostering understanding.[2]
- Finally, use appropriate humor, which can be an excellent de-escalator, especially if unexpected.

Other approaches to defuse a confrontation with the potential to escalate into a serious conflict include:

- Maintain a calm, confident attitude. Don't lose your temper; control your emotions.
- Speak in a quiet, firm, nonabrasive and nonthreatening manner.
- Allow the aggressor a way to "save face" or exit.
- Be straightforward if possible—obtaining willing cooperation is the best option.

Maintain calm and speak in a subdued manner. Constantly remind yourself, "This is not personal, it's not physically dangerous or threatening, I must continue to maintain my composure." To remain

---

2. Rivera, Luis. De-escalation; The Art of Avoiding Violence. Retrieved 09/16/17 from endesastres.org/files/The_best_way_to_deal_with_violence_is_to_avoid_it_1_.pdf

calm when others around you are being loud and argumentative calls for extraordinary presence of mind; focus on not letting temper and ego overrule common sense and training.

A conflict goes through five stages:

1. Conflict begins as a disagreement, misunderstanding, or total lack of communication. Each person tries to prevail and verbally beat the other into submission. During this phase, voices and body temperature begin to rise as though the argumentative participants believe the winner is the one who shouts the louder; reason and logic are thrown out as each side refuses to listen or cooperate with the other.
2. Either an agreement is reached or argument escalates to physical aggression, resulting in pushing, shoving, or fighting.
3. The third stage is a movement toward settlement or enforced cooperation.[3] In cases of noncompliance, it will eventually be settled on the side of the security team.
4. If the conflict and fight continue, they will evolve into use of nonlethal weapons.
5. If they continue further, they may include use of lethal weapons.

Another factor of importance is to act as if every action and word is being visually and audibly recorded. Choose your words and actions carefully so that you do not see yourself on the nightly news, the gossip blogs, or sitting in a courtroom.

POWER VERSUS FORCE

> Respect your efforts, respect yourself. Self-respect leads to self-discipline. When you have both firmly under your belt, that's real power.
> —Clint Eastwood

The power of a protective agent is inherently described by his position; while you won't have the power or authority of a law enforcement officer, often your position, combined with the degree of your

---

3. Rubin, Jeffrey, Z. (1993). Conflict from a psychological perspective. In Hall, Lavinia (1993). *Negotiation: Strategies for Mutual Gain.* Sage Publications, Thousand Oaks, CA, 1993, p. 124.

client's celebrity, offers a measure of implied authority. This alone may be sufficient to deter any adverse activity that you may encounter during an assignment. Power, or the illusion of it, may be all the strength needed to defuse a pushy fan or the overly rambunctious paparazzi.

> Power appeals to what uplifts, dignifies, and ennobles. Force must always be justified, whereas power requires no justification...Because force automatically creates counter-force, its effect is limited by definition. (It) could (be said) that force is a movement—it goes from here to there (or tries to) against opposition. Power, on the other hand is still. . . . Force always moves against something, whereas power doesn't move against anything at all. Force is incomplete and therefore has to be fed energy constantly. Power is total and complete in itself and requires nothing from outside.[4]

Facing a potential disruptive force like an uncooperative, noncompliant, and possibly mentally ill individual calls for an assertive response. The act of assertiveness requires effectively expressing one's own self and obtaining an understanding of the perspective of the aggressor while being respectful and gaining compliance. Being aggressive is attempting to reach agreement and compliance through the use of force, fear, or coercion. Aggressive communication or action can lead to a worsening of the circumstances, and so there is a very thin line between the assertive and the aggressive. In the heat of the moment, that line shrinks and quickly disappears. It is an emotionally and patiently strong person who can withstand the forces aligned against him or her to prevent transiting from assertive personality to aggressive anger.

SEXUAL HARASSMENT

The U.S. Equal Employment Opportunity Commission (EEOC) defines workplace sexual harassment as unwelcome sexual advances or conduct of a sexual nature that unreasonably interferes with the performance of a person's job or creates an intimidating, hostile, or offensive work environment.

---

4. Hawkins, David, R. (2002). *Power vs. Force, The Hidden Determinants of Human Behavior.* Carlsbad, CA: Hay House, p. 132.

As such, we all know that sexual harassment can occur in a variety of situations, but nowhere is it truer than in the entertainment industry. Examples of types of sexual harassment that the protector must be mindful of:

- Unwanted jokes, gestures, offensive words on clothing, and unwelcome comments and repartee that are sexual in nature.
- Touching and any other bodily contact, such as scratching or patting a coworker's back, grabbing an employee around the waist, kissing an employee, hugging an employee, or interfering with an employee's ability to move.
- Repeated requests for dates or other get-togethers that are turned down, or unwanted flirting.
- Transmitting or posting emails or pictures of a sexual or other harassment-related nature.
- Watching pornography or other suggestive material online or on smartphones even if the employee is watching in a private office.
- Displaying sexually suggestive objects, pictures, or posters in the workplace.[5]

(We note that this list is not intended to be all-inclusive, as so much of sexual harassment is in the perception of the victim.)

As mentioned earlier, assuming the role of protector to the beautiful and the famous comes complete with a variety of temptations on multiple levels, and while one might think of sexuality and the entertainment business as going hand-in-hand, we must try extremely hard to avoid even the perception of being involved in anything sexually inappropriate, as even an accusation can lead to life-altering problems.

Depending on the setting, there may be a time when you might be in proximity of the client when they are in various forms of undress. Perhaps it's a performance show and a quick-change area has been designated just offstage, or you may be on the set of a movie with a steamy scene being filmed. In those circumstances, it may be best to discretely turn around, avert your eyes or, if possible, leave the room. These are instances where the phrase "real world vs. textbook" applies. If the nature of the threat is unlikely to elevate during those

---

5. Retrieved 05/29/18 from https://www.thebalancecareers.com/sexual-harassment-1918253. Article appearing in Balanced Careers; Sexual Harassment—How to Prevent and Address Sexual Harassment in the Workplace; By Susan M. Heathfield (March 22, 2018).

moments, removing yourself from the station so that you do not make the VIP uncomfortable may actually keep you around in the long run so that you can protect them from the real threats down the road.

Because of the perceived power of a protective agent, there are many in the circle of celebrity who may wish to express their gratitude by offering sex as a reward. From a professional standpoint, this should be diplomatically declined, not only because of the moral issue, but because it will lessen the agent's power and professional focus and could create a hostile workplace if the circumstances change. In the age of the Me Too movement, what might have once been perceived as casual sexual innuendo, playful touches, or just jokes, can have devastating effects to both parties if unwelcomed. Consider well that if the remark or acts cause discomfort, this can be considered sexual harassment and can lead to serious trouble, of which being fired is the least.

Beginning in the last quarter of 2017, there were a number of sexual harassment accusations against many powerful and well-known respected male figures in the entertainment industry. Victims coming forward included several major A-list actresses who made claims of being exposed to male nudity, sexual innuendos, and coerced sex acts. While there may be very little a protector can do to prevent those acts behind closed doors, you might well find yourself drawn into the civil or criminal proceedings just by the nature of your role.

Chapter 13

CONCLUSION

Throughout this book, we have touched on a wide variety of topics as they relate to the celebrity protection industry, ranging from dealing with stalkers and paparazzi, to branding and communication skills. Our goal was to give the reader a peek behind the curtain to the many different facets of this industry. What you will find a lack of is an emphasis on the guns and ammo topics that seem to consume so much of the close protection discussion—even though they have very little to do with the actual job itself.

Additionally, we took great pains to not sugarcoat the various challenges that the protector will face, both operationally and ethically. Our hope is that this will be a guidebook that will inform, inspire, and educate the brave men and women who put in long, and often thankless, hours in the protection of others. Ours is a profession that stretches back through the centuries, and while it has had some blemishes from time to time, by and large, it is a career that will allow those who accept the calling and adhere to the true principals of the craft to hold their heads high.

Appendix

ADVANCE PROTECTIVE AGENT CHECKLISTS

No stone too small to turn over or rock too large to look under and nothing to overlook".

—Dale L. June

The following are examples of a protective agent's advance checklists and can be used as a basic reference; this list is not intended to be an "answer all." While additional elements can be added depending on the nature of the assignment, it will suffice as a guide or roadmap to a successful advance. It is expected that an advance agent will modify and edit any recommended checklist to match his or her own particular needs.

Things to do Before Departing for Assignment

1. Obtain name and telephone number of contact person.
2. Call contact person and make arrangements for meeting.
   a. Who is the host committee?
   b. Special dress requirements, if any?
   c. Types of expenses authorized?
   d. All pertinent phone numbers.
   e. Special requirements of principal
      i. Medical
      ii. Personal
      iii. Dietary
3. Determine types of functions principal will be attending—pack or dress accordingly.
4. Conduct office files and records check for previous advance reports to a particular location.
5. Check any special equipment including communications that might be required.
6. Check weather forecast for the area to be visited.

7. Conduct research of location to be visited (know local situation—history, location, political influence, crime and violence).
8. Determine billing arrangements—estimate amount of funds needed for the assignment.

Principal

1. Who is the principal?
    a. Be able to recognize him or her as well as members of his family and staff.
    b. Know the principal's itinerary.
    c. What time does he arrive?
    d. What time does he depart?
    e. Where is he visiting?
    f. What type of transportation is to be used?
    g. Who is providing?
    h. Who are the drivers or pilots?
    i. What is their training?
    j. Phone numbers?
    k. Language considerations?
2. Will an interpreter be needed for the principal?
3. Will an interpreter be needed for the security detail?
4. Medical problems of the principal or members of his party.
5. Amount of baggage expected.

Arrival at Site/City of Visit

1. Observe the general layout of the airport.
2. Obtain a good map of the area and orient yourself in general terms.
3. Obtain rental vehicle.
4. Proceed to your hotel and observe:
    a. Traffic conditions
    b. Road conditions
    c. General topography
    d. Landmarks
    e. Time and distance
    f. Check into hotel and note:
        i. Parking areas
        ii. Lobby configuration
        iii. Elevator locations
        iv. Service elevators
        v. Areas of congestion

        vi. Restaurant locations
        vii. Other amenities
5. Contact your home office:
   a. Tell them where you are and how to contact you.
   b. Inquire as to any changes.
   c. Obtain messages.
   d. Check in with your home office at least once per day.
6. Make preliminary telephone contact with:
   a. The local contact for the visit (Host)
   b. The hotel
        i. Resident manager, reservations manager, or assistant manager
        ii. Have reservations been made for security detail as well as principal's party?
        iii. Number of agents authorized per room
   c. If other than a hotel, is there adequate room to lodge the security detail and to set up a Command Post?
   d. Auto rental agency or limousine company if vehicles are needed
        i. Drivers and/or Pilots
        ii. Where are they staying?
        iii. Contact Numbers?
   e. Police
7. Intelligence
   a. Threat Assessments
   b. Dangerous People file
8. Motorcade advice
9. Special problems
10. Road construction or closings
11. Special events
12. Emergency and nonemergency direct telephone numbers

SITE SURVEYS

The investigation and resultant plans of security for a given location generally involves all security measures taken at a place to be visited by the principal, in order to identify undesirable elements and physical hazards. Once these are identified, you can take necessary action to reduce risk or harm to the principal. Conducting a site survey is comparable to any complete, thorough, professional criminal investigation, including looking for clues of countersurveillance or adverse activity, but primary attention is given to factors either embarrassing or harmful to the principal.

1. Contact person(s) in charge of the area or site (key contact person)
   a. Building manager or owner.
   b. Evaluate area where event is to occur.
   c. Consider the time that the principal will be exposed.
   d. Examine factors that are difficult to control:
      i. Crowds
      ii. Location
      iii. Press sites
      iv. Items outside the secured area
      v. Vehicles parked nearby
      vi. Buildings across the street
      vii. Woodlands and parks
      viii. Curious passersby
      ix. Bridges, overpasses, tunnels, manholes, parked cars
2. Check all travel times and distances involved.
3. Check and evaluate all emergency data:
   a. Emergency phone numbers
   b. Equipment on hand
   c. Emergency escape routes
   d. Extra motorcade
   e. Panic bars, stairwells, locks, all doors, etc.
4. Decide on identification:
   a. Security team members
   b. Principal's staff
   c. Others in entourage
   d. Host committee
   e. Press area
   f. General public and general holding room
5. Determine personnel and logistical needs:
   a. Establish security posts
   b. Route surveys
   c. Determine safety hazards
   d. Improper lighting
   e. Inadequate emergency exits
   f. Overcrowding
   g. Faulty equipment
   h. Elevators (lock down elevators, make one express; others stop on floor below)
   i. Podium, lectern, lighting, microphones, visual aids, chairs, etc.
   j. Delay problems that could hinder rapid movement of principal
6. Preventive measures
   a. Provide buffer zones between principal and public.

b. Control limited access areas.
   c. Screen all things entering a secured area after a sweep.
   d. Change and control untenable situations.
   e. Control movement of the principal.
   f. Reduce principal's exposure.
   g. Effect continuity of security:
      i. Health hazards
      ii. Smoke
      iii. Fumes
      iv. Water
      v. Food
      vi. Heating and air conditioning
      vii. Electric blankets, grounded lamps, etc.

Types of Security Surveys

1. Airports
2. Ballrooms
3. Auditoriums
4. Hotels
5. Coliseums (Stadiums)
6. Private residences
7. Office buildings, factories, etc.
8. Routes of travel
9. Outdoor activities

Basic Perimeter Security Theory

1. Where is the principal?
   a. Home
   b. Work
   c. Airplane
   d. Concert
   e. Golf course
   f. Sports event
2. Who else is at that location?
   a. Immediate family
   b. A few trusted friends
   c. General public
   d. Members of government
   e. Spectators at a sporting event
   f. Other persons who attract controversy or have high risk profiles

3. Was there advance notice?
   a. Publicity
   b. Press
   c. Invitations
4. What time of day?
5. Weather conditions?
6. Proximity of people to the principal:
   a. Banquet
   b. Golf tournament
   c. Parade, Handshaking, Reception
7. What intelligence do you have?
   a. General
   b. Specific
8. How will the "Rings of protection" be deployed?

Things to Consider While Developing Plans

1. What technical equipment do you need, have access to, or can get to your location?
   a. Portable alarm systems
   b. CCTV (cameras and monitors)
   c. Bulletproof vests
   d. Armored vehicles
   e. Global positioning systems
   f. Computers
   g. Bomb and metal detectors
   h. Night vision equipment
   i. Communications equipment
   j. Firearms
2. What is the lay of the land?
   a. Tall buildings
   b. Mountains
   c. Flat fields
   d. Woodlands with brush and shrubs
   f. Ocean, lake, or river
3. How many people are available for post standing and other assignments?
   a. How well trained are they?
   b. How experienced are they?
4. What is the timeframe for preparation?
5. How much protection will the principal require?

Appendix

HOTEL ADVANCE

Walk and learn the hotel prior to meeting with the hotel staff, and if you have special requests, meet with the hotel manager. If the visit requires the special services of housekeeping, food service, security, etc., set up a meeting with the hotel manager and department heads (meet all at same time if possible). Have your requests printed, and hand them out in the presence of the hotel manager. It is important to have solutions to their objections.

Principal's Suite

1. Conduct a thorough examination of the suite.
2. The principal's suite should be located away from the elevators and stairwells.
3. Know what is above, below, and adjacent to the suite.
4. Attempt to occupy these rooms with the protective detail or staff.
5. The suite should not be accessible from common balconies of fire escapes.
6. The suite should not be accessible for adjacent buildings.
7. It is recommended that the suite be located above the 1st and below the 6th floor in the event of fire.
8. Rooms with a false ceiling or other areas where listening devices or explosives could be concealed should be avoided.
9. Special needs or requests should be verified:
   a. King-size bed
   b. Bar
   c. DVD
   d. Video games
   e. Refrigerator
   f. Color scheme
   g. Cleanliness
   h. View

Command Post

1. The Command Post should be close to, but not immediately next to, the principal's suite.
2. It should be located between the general traffic areas and the principal's suite.

Hotel Services

1. Determine the location and availability of all hotel services.
2. Have room service and all deliveries for the principal's suite delivered to the command post or agent's room for inspection and delivery.
3. Command post or agent should order the principal's food without disclosing to the kitchen the intended recipient.

Fire System

1. How does it work?
2. When was the alarm activation last tested?
3. Is the report verified before sounding the alarm?
4. You are not planning on staying during an alarm.
5. Check fire equipment on floor:
    a. Fire extinguishers
    b. Water hoses
    c. Emergency exits

Other Hotel Advance Considerations

1. Has the hotel been announced as the temporary residence?
2. Is the main function of the principal at the hotel where the principal is staying?
3. Principal should be registered under a false name.

Hotel Advance

1. Meet with:
    a. Resident Manager
    b. General Manager
2. Determine who will be your working contact.
3. Get names, hotel, and home phone numbers of all main people:
    a. General Manager
    b. Head Chef
    c. Food & Beverage Manager
    d. Catering (Room Service)
    e. Room Reservation Manager
    f. Banquet Manager
    g. Head Housekeeper
    h. Chief Hotel Telephone Operator
    i. Security Manager

j. Day & Night Manager
k. Concierge
l. Public Relations Manager
m. Transportation Manager
n. Maintenance & Engineering Manager
o. House Physician

Make a Thorough Examination of the Principal's Suite

1. Location and security problems:
   a. What is above and below?
   b. What is on either side?
   c. Choose a suite far removed from elevators and stairwells
   d. Access to suite from lobby
   e. False ceilings
   f. Age of building and floor level
   g. Isolated area
   h. No common balconies
   i. No exposure to adjacent buildings
   j. Are there curtains and/or blinds to cover windows?
   k. No outside fire escape vulnerabilities
   l. Is the suite more than one level?
   m. Determine Command Post location:
       i. Same floor
       ii. Close proximity to the suite
2. Select rooms for the balance of the principal's party and the security detail
   a. Above, below, and beside the principal's suite
   b. Take the whole floor or wing of suites if possible.
   c. If possible, get the names of other guests within the perimeter.
   d. Check rooms for problems.

Meeting with Rooms Reservation Manager

1. Block rooms in one secured area.
2. Arrange billings.
3. Obtain suite and C.P. keys.
4. Arrange to pre-register.
5. Arrange to have all reserved room keys at the C.P. on arrival.
6. Arrange to check bills after departure of party.
7. Arrange for extra stand-by rooms.
8. Arrange to have beds removed from the C.P.
9. Any other special arrangements.

Meeting with Assistant Manager and Security Chief

1. Request names of people who will need access to the suite. Keep list to a minimum. Post the list in C.P. Always accompany them into the suite.
   a. Room Service
   b. Waiters, caterers
   c. Maids
   d. Bell Captain, Bellboys
   e. Valet
   f. Baggage handlers
2. Request blocked parking areas for vehicles, preferably in view of the parking attendant, guard, etc.
3. Know how to operate the elevators. Request express elevators for arrivals and departures.
4. Get the phone numbers for the persons who will operate the elevators.
   a. When were elevators last inspected?
   b. Who will respond to stuck elevators?
5. Arrange to order food service through one or two contacts.
   a. Always have food delivered to the C.P. or staff person's room.
   b. Arrange for tips.
6. Arrange baggage handlers with carts for arrivals and departures.
7. Determine emergency power source and emergency lighting.
8. If possible, get a radio from hotel security or their radio frequency.
9. Always have alternate exits and entrances.
10. Arrange coffee, soft drinks, and midnight snacks for C.P.
11. Ascertain hotel staff and services available. Get names and numbers.
    a. Masseuse
    b. Barber or Beautician
    c. Shoeshine, laundry or dry cleaning
    d. Clothing store
    e. Drugstore
    f. Health club
    g. Get copies of all hotel restaurant menus.
    h. Ascertain room service hours and have them extended if necessary.
    i. Arrange for gifts, packages, etc. to be delivered to the C.P.
    j. Obtain floor plan and diagrams of hotel for C.P.
12. Ascertain when they last had a fire inspection. Inspect it yourself.
13. Ask to see copies of the security incident reports or at least get an idea of the types of security problems they have had in the past.

14. Find out what other events are scheduled to take place at the hotel.
15. Check stairwells for lighting, obstacles, doors, etc.
16. Do not list the principal's suite number as belonging to him/her.
17. Brief chief hotel operators on how to handle calls to the principal's suite.
    a. Do not reveal suite number.
    b. Route all calls via staff, then to the C.P.—not to the suite directly.
    c. Advise C.P. of threat or bomb calls.
18. Ascertain if hotel security is armed, how to contact them, and how to identify them. Try and get a sense of their training and when they make their rounds.
19. Determine hotel's policy as to demonstrators, hecklers, and people who interfere with guests.
20. Know the best nearby hospitals and their routes.
21. Ascertain who will greet the principal—approved photographers?
22. Make sure the greeting is inside, preferably on the suite floor.
23. Can the principal have kitchen privileges?
24. Keep good records of people who have helped you out, and later send thank-you notes.
25. Select agent posts:
    a. Checkpoints
    b. Suite post
    c. Command Post
    d. Roving patrols
    e. Surveillance

Command Post Equipment

1. Radios, chargers and batteries
2. Flashlights
3. Fire extinguisher
4. Gas mask or fire/smoke escape mask
5. Shoulder weapons
6. Medical kit
7. Keys to the principal's suite
8. Vehicle keys and locations
9. Itinerary
10. General instructions
11. Special instructions
12. Motorcade configurations
13. Emergency telephone numbers
14. Hospitals (maps, route directions, telephone numbers, doctors on duty)

15. Fire Dept. (representative and telephone numbers of contacts)
16. Police Dept. (representative and telephone numbers of contacts)
17. Ambulance Service (paramedics and physicians)
18. Room assignment list
19. Telephone list of all contacts
20. Name lists of all authorized personnel
21. Diagrams of site
22. Intelligence information
23. Route maps to all locations to be visited by principal
24. Alternate routes
25. Emergency hospital and evacuation information
26. Principal's dossier
    a. Forms for agents
    b. Posted fire evacuation routes and plan with diagrams of hotel

ROUTE SURVEY

Route surveys need to include the following information:
1. Considerations in choosing routes
    a. What is the date and time that the route is to be used?
    b. Holidays—different traffic flow
    c. Weekends—different traffic flow
    d. Near factories, government buildings, schools, major entertainment facilities?
    e. What are the shift changes or when crowds are released?
    f. Train tracks
    g. Bridges, tunnels
    h. Overpasses, underpasses
    i. Construction areas
    j. Special events, parades, demonstrations, sporting events
    k. Parks and wooded areas
    l. How many intersections, stop lights and stop signs?
    m. Number of buildings and windows
    n. Storage areas, mailboxes, sidewalk obstructions
    o. Pedestrian traffic
    p. Hospitals, police stations, fire stations, medical facilities, etc.
2. Detailed routes should be completed with accompanying map or route cards.
3. Alternate routes should be completed in detail with accompanying maps or route cards.
4. Time and date survey conducted.

AIRPORT SECURITY SURVEYS

1. Persons to Contact
   a. Airline services representative
      i. Is there a private airline VIP room or club available for your principal's use?
      ii. Determine which gate the flight will be arriving and departing from.
      iii. Arrange for principal to board first or last and have priority deboarding.
      iv. Make arrangements for the principal and security teams' baggage to be loaded last and taken off first.
      v. Special menu arrangements
      vi. Special seating arrangements
   b. Airport police/security representative/airport authority
      i. Obtain a layout of the terminal
      ii. Find the locations of:
         1. Restrooms
         2. Medical facilities
         3. Telephones
         4. Gift shops
         5. Restaurants
         6. Duty-free shopping
         7. Shoeshine
         8. Barber
         9. Departure gates & VIP lounges
      iii. Arrange for escort privileges in restricted areas.
      iv. Arrange for plane-side boarding and deboarding of principal.
      v. Arrange for motorcade parking.
      vi. Obtain whatever intelligence information available on possible threats.
      vii. Arrange assistance in clearing Customs and Immigration.
2. Identify the location of the nearest hospital.
3. Complete primary and alternate route surveys to and from the airports.
4. Have a contingency plan in the event that the scheduled flight is canceled.
5. Arrange for plane security if travel is by private plane.

BANQUETS, BALLROOMS, AND AUDITORIUMS

1. Contact the host or sponsor and get the following information:
   a. Who are the banquet manager, caterer, facility manager and host committee?
   b. Obtain phone numbers, including off-hours numbers. Also, give them your contact numbers.
2. Obtain a diagram or blueprint of the facility, and a diagram and seating chart for the function.
3. Note evacuation routes, location of alarms and fire-fighting apparatus, and access control points.
4. Arrange to have awards, trophies, etc. inspected and/or mailed to your principal at a later date.
5. How is admission to be handled?
   a. Open, general or reserved tickets?
   b. What is the price of admission and what do the tickets look like?
   c. Invitation only: are invitations serialized and registered?
   d. Are guests checked off as they arrive?
   e. Are substitutions permitted or possible?
   f. Where are the access control points and who will man them?
   g. Will the facility be providing security at the event? If so, get details.
   h. What is the itinerary of the event, and what part does your principal play?
   i. Will the lights go out at any time during the event for movies, slides, etc.?
   j. Check the seating arrangement. Who is around your principal?
   k. Arrange for seating for the agents.
6. Will there be media coverage?
   a. Who is responsible for handling the media?
   b. Make sure they are channeled into a secure area, and check press passes.
   c. Assign one room as a media/press room for interviews.
   d. TV crews may have problems because of the amount of equipment. A good working knowledge of their needs regarding shots, lighting, access, etc., is very helpful.
7. Who is responsible for backstage areas and security?
   a. Who has backstage privileges?
   b. Who issues and checks backstage passes?
8. Who is responsible for utilities, air conditioning, hearing, lighting, etc.?
   a. Is there an engineer on site and on duty?
   b. Are the control panels lockable and tamper-proof?

9. What dress will be required (business attire, black tie, etc.)?
10. Is there an arrival point for the principal? Can you bypass the main access point?
11. Can you get vehicles close to the stage for bussing/de-bussing?
    a. Where will vehicles be parked?
    b. Is there security for the vehicle during the event?
    c. Where can you stash a backup vehicle?
12. Is there a holding room? Secured rest rooms?
13. What type of stage is it?
    a. Foldable?
    b. Make sure that the stage, tables, and chair legs and supports are fully extended and locked to prevent injury or embarrassment.
    c. Are there loose wires?
    d. What type of curtains? Are they secure?
    e. Look overhead for potential hazards. Check catwalks.
    f. Look under the stage for potential hazards and trap doors.
    g. Check the stage for nails, loose carpets, etc.
    h. What types of barriers are around the stage?
        i. Plants
        ii. Trees
        iii. Velvet ropes
14. Post selection
    a. Do agents have good observation perspectives?
    b. Meals? Will the agents be relieved for eating?
15. Who are the waiters for the head table?
    a. When where they hired?
    b. Arrange for the waiters serving the head table to be provided with special pins, scarves, etc. for identification.
    c. Get names and addresses of head table staff and all other waiters if possible.
16. Physically walk the layout of the facility.
    a. Note dark areas near stairways, walkways, etc. Bring a flashlight for dark areas that your principal may be moving through.
    b. Look for and check out vending machines along the route.
    c. Look for places where persons could hide or doorways that could be opened suddenly, including doors marked Electric, Danger, or Do Not Enter.
17. Note the location of medical facilities and the location of the nearest hospital.
18. Prepare for possible demonstrations and be aware that many large outside demonstrations are diversions to draw resources away from a demonstrator who may sneak inside the event.

RESTAURANTS

1. Obtain the following information and note the location of:
   a. Telephones
   b. Restrooms
   c. Emergency exits—and note where the emergency exits open to
   d. Kitchen
   e. Parking
   f. Fire extinguishers
2. Prepare a diagram of the locations of the above.
3. Select safe seating (away from doorways, windows, etc.).
   a. If you have a choice, select a table with easy access to a side exit, and ask if you can enter the restaurant from that side.
   b. An agent will usually not sit at the same table as the principal, but will sit at a table inside that provides a good view of the access points and possible paths of attack to the principal.
4. Check for access control, and have an agent near each point, if possible.
5. Obtain a copy of the menu for the principal in advance.
6. If possible, avoid going through kitchens with the principal, as kitchens have many hazards such as slippery floors, etc.
7. Whenever possible and practical, call in the team member's food order before arriving. Order food that can be easily prepared, eaten quickly, and is not messy.
8. Arrange for team members to be served before the principal.
9. Make sure to feed your drivers. They should not eat inside the vehicles, as they could spill and the odor will linger.
10. Arrange for billing and tipping to be taken care of early by a team member.
11. Make sure that the Maitre D', Chef, Head Waiter, Waiter, Bus Staff, and Wine Steward are properly tipped.
12. Notify other team members of any change in plans, the next destination, and when the client will depart.
13. Notify the drivers well in advance of departure, so they can have the vehicles warmed up and in position for pickup.

OUTDOOR EVENTS

1. Check for the following information:
   a. What is the weather forecast?
   b. What is the impact of bad weather?

2. Will there be a tent or other covered area?
    a. If so, are all lines, fasteners, pegs, and poles secured?
    b. How will the covered area be exited?
    c. What will you do if it collapses or is tampered with?
    d. Are there outdoor space heaters?
        i. Are they secured and won't tip over?
        ii. When will they be turned on?
        iii. Are the heaters gas, oil, or electric?

TEAM MOVEMENT (ON FOOT OR VEHICLE)

1. Is movement formal or informal?
2. Are the route and time predictable?
3. Is the route the shortest one possible?
4. Does it provide minimum exposure?
5. Is there an alternate route available?
6. Where are the danger points?
7. What is the best evacuation route in the event of an emergency?
8. Is there a safe area available?
9. Where is the nearest medical facility, and what is the best route to it?
10. Are there any physical hazards such as construction sites, bad footing, vicious dogs, overhead balconies, etc.?
11. What types of formations are best suited for the movement?
12. Are barriers needed for crowd control?
13. What support is available or needed from other security/law enforcement services?
14. Number, type, and location of security posts?
15. Are there direct communications with the Command Post and the site or motorcade?
16. What special equipment will be needed?
17. How many people will accompany the principal during movements?

TEAM BRIEFING

Team Leader

The team leader is responsible for the team briefing after receiving all necessary information. In some circumstances, the advance man is responsible for the briefing. The briefing is an exercise in coordination around the principal's schedule.

Team Briefing Format

1. Roll call
2. Introduction—make sure everyone on the team knows each other by name and recognition.
3. Introduce supervisors and other key personnel.
4. Principal
    a. Name, title, how should they be addressed
    b. Picture of principal and family members, staff
    c. Reason for visit
    d. Biographic data on principal
    e. Medical history of principal
        i. Blood type
        ii. Allergies
        iii. Health problems
        iv. Special requirements or equipment needed
        v. Is the personal physician traveling with principal?
5. Itinerary for visit
    a. Supervisors should be given copies
    b. Arrival times and locations
    c. Departure times and locations
    d. Traveling party entourage or accompanying staff, with their titles and responsibilities
    e. Name of the contact person
6. Security in Party
    a. Is principal traveling with their own security?
    b. Are they armed?
    c. How many?
    d. How are they identified?
    e. Where will they ride in the motorcade?
    f. Who is in charge of the principal's security team?
    g. Who has final responsibility for the principal?
7. Intelligence & Threat Assessment
    a. General intelligence
    b. Specific intelligence
    c. Countersurveillance
8. EOD Operations
9. Detail Operations
    a. Close protection detail
    b. Post assignments
        i. Report time
        ii. Relief/quit time

10. Communications
    a. Radio frequencies
    b. Telephone numbers
        i. Landlines
        ii. Cellular telephones
    c. Codes
        i. Ten codes
        ii. Duress codes
        iii. Passwords
        iv. Route codes
        v. Hand signals
11. Identification
    a. Lapel or other security identification pins
    b. Descriptions
    c. Other staff members
    d. Event staff
    e. Host committee
    f. Visitors
    g. Law enforcement and security (armed and unarmed)
12. Transportation
13. Location of safe areas and holding rooms
14. Logistics and Administration
15. Special Instructions
16. Attachments
    a. Route sheets
    b. Route cards
    c. Maps
    d. Diagrams and drawings
    e. Photos
    f. Telephone numbers

HOSPITAL SITE SURVEY

Operation name:_____ Date:_____

Case control number:_____

Hospital name: _____

Address:_____

Phone number:_____

Contacts

Administration: _____

Office phone: _____

Cell phone: _____

Security: _____

Office phone: _____

Cell phone: _____

Building Maintenance: _____

Office phone: _____

Cell phone: _____

Public Affairs (Press Office): _____

Office phone: _____

Cell phone: _____

Additional recommendations:

_____

_____

Details

Hospital description:

_____

_____

_____

Hours of operation: _____

Surrounding area description (rural/suburban/urban) and cross streets:

_____

_____

Trauma center level:_____

Patient type description: _____

Map of area, including major streets and highways:

Additional recommendations:

_____

_____

_____

Security

Security staff:

    Armed ___   K-9 ___

    Unarmed ___   Vehicle Patrol ___

    Static posts ___

    Total number of officers:_____

    Shift hours:_____   _____ _____

    Number of officers on shift:_____

Shift supervisor's name: _____

Phone number: _____

    Name: _____ Phone number: _____

    Name: _____ Phone number: _____

Radio frequency: _____

Radio availability: _____ Amount: _____

Radio and cellular dead zones: _____

Security Cameras: Recorded:

    If so, how long: _____

    Monitored 24/7: If not, hours monitored: _____

Describe camera coverage:

_____

_____

Availability of Safe Room in or near security offices (Y/N): _____

Safe Room location: _____

Safe Room access secured (Y/N): _____

Map to Security Office and Safe Room:

Police

Local Police Department: _____

Police Department address: _____

Phone numbers:

Dispatch (nonemergency): _____

Watch Commander:

    Desk: _____

    Cellular: _____

Intelligence Unit: _____

Joint Terrorism Task Force contact: _____

Response time to hospital: _____

Safe Haven (Y/N): _____

Map to Police Department:

Additional recommendations:

_____

_____

Fire Department

Local Fire Department: _____

Fire Department address: _____

Phone numbers _____

Dispatch (nonemergency): _____

Fire Captain:

    Desk: _____

    Cellular: _____

Paramedics: _____

Life Flight capability: _____

Life Flight phone number: _____

Private ambulance phone number: _____

Response time to hospital: _____

Safe Haven (Y/N): _____

Map to Fire Department:

Additional recommendations:

_____

_____

Emergency Room

Location within hospital: _____

Contact phone numbers:

☐ _____

☐ _____

☐ _____

☐ _____

☐ _____

Available equipment:

☐ _____

☐ _____

☐ _____

☐ _____

☐ _____

☐ _____

☐ _____

Triage Area ___

Resuscitation Area ___

Pediatric Area ___

Primary Language (OCONUS): _____

Blood types available: _____ _____ _____

Map to ER:

Additional recommendations:
_____

_____

Parking Areas

Description:_____

Security Booth: ___   Lighting: ___

Gate: ___   Fencing: ___

Card Access: ___   Vehicle Barriers: ___

Security patrols: ___

Arrival and departure area for protectee (Y/N):___ Secure (Y/N):___

Description:
_____

_____

Map of parking area:

Additional recommendations:
_____

_____

Perimeter of Hospital (Interior-Exterior)

Lighting: Door descriptions: _____

Fence line: Lock descriptions: _____

Barbed obstacle topping:

Vehicle standoff distances:_____

_____

Alarms: _____ Doors: _____

Windows: _____

Patients alarmed: _____

Additional recommendations:

_____

_____

Overall Security and Disaster Preparedness

Roof security: _____

Ventilation security: _____

Below-ground security: _____

Electrical panels security: _____

Backup generator: _____

Location:_____

Water security: _____

Natural gas line (Y/N):____ Shutoff valve security:_____

Emergency lighting (Y/N): _____

Disaster evacuation procedures:

_____

_____

Location of disaster survival kits:

_____

Location of fire extinguishers:

_____

Location of AEDs: _____

Correctional inmate security wing (Y/N): _____

Evacuation rally area (map):

Additional recommendations:

_____

_____

Employees

Training:

Medical:

_____

_____

Security:_____

Appendix 195

Disaster: _____

Uniforms:

Uniform description and photos:

_____

_____

Identification badge description and photos:

_____

_____

Additional recommendations:

_____

_____

INDEX

A

Advance surveys, 82–85. *See also* Checklists; Security surveys
Aggression, 163
Airport security surveys, 179
Assertiveness, 17, 133, 163
Attacks on Principals (AOP), 110, 114–115, 119–120. *See also* Stalking

B

Back of house (BOH) security, 42–43
Bardo-Schaffer attack, 7
Bieber, Justin, 114–115
Black, Laura, 120–122
Blogs, 153–155. *See also* Social media
Body mechanics, 102–103, 132
Bodyguards. *See also* Checklists
  anticipation, planning, and preparation, 82–83, 121–122, 141, 149–151
  coping with long hours, 47–49, 66
  historical overview of, 9
  job description and exceptions, 79–81
  niche work for, 11–16, 42–43
  phases in the profession of, 21
  power *vs.* force used by, 162–163
  protective services *vs.*, 159–163
  terminology options, 15–16
  training for, 5, 61–62
  wardrobe and appearance of, 23–24, 30, 136–137, 151
Brand protection, 130, 141, 149, 153, 156–157
Bremer, Arthur, 113
Burnout, 68

C

Cardinal virtues, 54–55
Cary, Mariah, 139
Celebrities
  contrasted to executive protection, 21–22, 27, 49, 53, 76
  instant fame of, 78–79
  narcissism in, 75–76
  operating in their world, 28–29
  protection needs of, 4, 6–7
  protector's knowledge about, 27–28, 30, 56, 85
  public accessibility to, 81–82
  revenue stream of, 41, 156
  schedules of, 76–78
  stalking of, 7, 114–115
  worship of, 115–117
Checklists. *See also* Advance surveys; Security surveys
  airport security surveys, 179
  banquets, ballrooms and auditoriums, 180–181
  basic perimeter security theory, 171
  before departing for assignment, 167–169
  hospital site surveys, 185–195
  hotel advance surveys, 173–178
  outdoor event surveys, 182
  planning considerations, 172
  restaurant advance surveys, 182
  route surveys, 178
  site surveys, 169–171
  team briefing, 183–185
  team movement (on foot or vehicle), 183
Citizen's arrest, 159

Close personal protection (CPP), 103. *See also* Executive protection
Cognitive thinking, 33
Communication skills
   de-escalation techniques, 160–162
   educating celebrities, 158
   expectations regarding, 25
   requisite, 34, 137
   usefulness of, 134
   verbal judo, 46, 46nn1–3
   with fans, 133, 148, 151
Conflict, stages of, 162
Cooper, Jeff, 36
Corporate protection. *See* Executive protection
Counterfeited passes, 142, 145
Courtesy, 29–30
Cover and Evacuation, 109
Crashers, 145–147. *See also* Fans
Credentials, 141–143, 145
Critical thinking, 18, 18n2, 31

D

De-escalation techniques, 160–162
Delegation, 80–81
Dietz, Park E., 111
Douglas, Michael, 115
Drivers, 87, 94–95, 98

E

Elevator pitches, 14
Embussing and debussing vehicles, 96
Erotomania, 113
Ethics, 54–56
Event security
   backstage crashers, 145–146
   festival crashers, 146–147
   limiting and controlling access, 141–143
   pass types, 142–145
   protector placement at, 140–141
   securing the stage, 148–149
   signing sessions, 149–152
   staff at, 139–140, 142, 149–150
Executive protection. *See also* Close personal protection (CPP)
   client profile, 23
   overview of, 9, 22–25
   resource about, 7
   social media and, 119
   vs. celebrity, 21–22, 27, 49, 53, 76
Exercises to improve observation skills, 33

F

Fans. *See also* Crashers
   at Red Carpet events, 131–134
   celebrity worship by, 115–117
   obsessive, 117–119
   photos with, 132–133, 151
   protectees interacting with, 126f
   protectors communicating with, 133, 148, 151
   stalkers, 110–115
   types of, 6–7
Farley, Richard, 120–122
Festivals, 146–147
Film resources. *See* Marketing
Film world
   absence from family, 67–69
   advance surveys for, 82–84 (*See also* Checklists)
   anticipation, planning, and preparation, 82–83, 121–122
   award shows, 65–66
   cloning the protector, 84
   location shoots, 65
   personalities and bosses, 66–67
   safety and security compromises, 69–72
   security surveys, 85–86
   studio shoots, 63–65
   tedium in, 66
Force *vs.* power, 162–163
Foster, Jody, 113
Four Square app, 118

G

Geo-tagging, 118–119
Governmental protection, 9
Grimmie, Christina Victoria, 119–120

H

Health issues, 64, 68–69, 116
Hinckley, John, 113
Honey trap, 50
Hospital site surveys, 185–195
Hotel advance surveys, 173–178

I

ICON Training Academy, 3, 5
Imagination, 31–32
Interpersonal politics, 45–46
Interviewing section at Red Carpet events, 130–131
Introduction to Executive Protection (June), 7

L

Law enforcement
    protective services *vs.*, 159–163
    support from, 97, 122, 150
    training, 18, 34, 36
Legislation relevant to security, 7, 121
Loibl, Kevin, 119–120

M

Madonna, 114
Marketing. *See also* Protection profession as a business
    elevator pitches, 14
    image creation, 14–15
    management agencies, 57–59
    movie studios, 73
    networking, 61–62, 66, 135
    niche work, 11–16, 42–43
    production companies, 73–75
    publicists, 60–61
    record companies, 59–60
    talent agencies, 73
Meals, 30, 39–40, 64. *See also* Nutrition
Media interactions, 153–158
Mental health concerns, 69, 116
Military training, 18, 34
Mindset, 32
Morals and ethical dilemmas, 54–56
Motorcades, 96–98
Mullen, Paul, 112–113
Music resources. *See* Marketing
Music world
    challenging clients in, 52–54
    coping with long hours, 47–49, 66
    dealing with temptations, 50–51
    giving and receiving gifts, 56–57
    morals and ethical dilemmas, 54–56
    personal appearances, 43–44
    personal time, 45
    photo shoots, 44–45
    recording process, 38–41
    touring, 41–43
    working away from home, 52
    working with the entourage, 45–47

N

Narcissism in celebrities, 75–76
Networking, 61, 66, 135. *See also* Marketing
News programs, 153–154. *See also* Press *vs.* paparazzi
Nixon, Richard, 113
Nutrition, 64. *See also* Health issues; Meals

O

Observation, 32–33, 107
Oil stains, 93
Oracle, 119
Outdoor event surveys, 182

P

Paltrow, Gwyneth, 115
Paparazzi, 6, 6n2, 95–96, 128–130, 153–158
Pass types, 142–145
Personal appearances by celebrities, 43–44
Perspective, 32
Photos and photo shoots, 44–45, 155–156
Police. *See* Law enforcement
Positioning and walking with clients. *See also* Red Carpet events
    body language, 101
    body mechanics, 102–103
    moving the client, 103–108
    preventing problems, 108
    reacting to threats, 108–109
    stalking, 110–111, 117
    sub-categories of stalkers, 112–113
Power *vs.* force used by bodyguards, 162–163
Press *vs.* paparazzi, 155–158. *See also* News stories
Production staff, 137
Protection profession as a business. *See also* Marketing
    benefits of, 5
    distinguishing oneself in, 12–13
    elevator pitches, 14

niches in, 11–16, 42–43
terminology options for, 15–16
Protective intelligence and assessment, 118, 121–122
Protective services *vs.* law enforcement, 159–163
Purpose and principles of protection
  age factor, 25
  attitude, 33–34
  blending in, 23–24
  business norms and practices, 24–25
  communication skills, 25, 34
  corporate protection, 22–25
  executive *vs.* celebrity, 21–22, 27
  flexibility, 34–35
  imagination, 31–32
  job candidacy, 18–19
  know your role, 26–27, 30, 126f
  knowing your client, 27–28, 30
  mental characteristics of protectors, 20–21, 30–31
  observation, 32–33, 107
  operating in their world, 28–29
  perspective, 32
  physical characteristics of protectors, 19–20
  positions of power, 26
  security principles, 17, 103
  situational awareness in, 36
  spatial awareness in, 36–37
  staying engaged, 35

R

Red Carpet events. *See also* Positioning and walking with clients
  Arm's Length Away philosophy, 125f, 127f
  fans at, 131–134
  interviewing section at, 130–131
  overview of, 123, 128
  photographers at, 128–130
  seating at, 125f, 134–138
Reflex reactions, 33
Restaurant advance surveys, 182
Restraining orders, 115, 120, 122
Route surveys, 178

S

Schaffer, Rebecca, 7
Seat fillers, 136–137
Security escorts, 106, 127f
Security surveys, 85–86. *See also* Advance surveys; Checklists
Selection criteria for protection professionals, 18–19
Self-monitoring, 162
Seven deadly sins, 54–55
Sexual harassment, 163–165
Site surveys, 169–171
Situational awareness, 36
Social media
  anonymity of, 114
  as protective intelligence, 117–119, 121
  blogs, 153–155
  prevalence of, 153
  stalking behaviors on, 111
Spatial awareness, 36–37
Stage security, 148–149
Stalking, 7, 110–115, 117–121. *See also* Attacks on principals (AOP)
Swag, 50
Swift, Taylor, 115

T

Tardiness, 93
Team concept, 4, 183–185
Tour buses, 99–100, 124f
Touring, 41–43, 124f
Training, 5, 61–62
Transportation preparations, 89–92

V

Vehicle Dynamics Institute (VDI), 98
Vehicles
  checklist of features to know, 89–92
  door opening, 94
  drivers, 87, 94–95, 98
  embussing and debussing, 96
  emergency equipment, 91–92
  motorcades, 96–98
  moving in and out of cars, 93

protector placement in, 92, 99
specialty, 88–89
standard, 87–88
tour buses, 99–100
Verbal judo, 46, 46nn1–3

W

Wallace, George, 113

Worship of celebrities, 115–117
Wranglers, 136–137

Z

Zero presence, 23
Zeta-Jones, Catherine, 115